Brain Power

Also by Catherine de Lange

10 Voyages Through the Human Mind

Brain Power

Everything You Need
to Know for a Healthy,
Happy Brain

Catherine de Lange

Michael O'Mara Books Limited

For Alok

This paperback edition first published in 2024
First published in Great Britain in 2022 by
Michael O'Mara Books Limited
9 Lion Yard
Tremadoc Road
London SW4 7NQ

A CIP catalogue record for this book is available from the British Library.

Papers used by Michael O'Mara Books Limited are natural, recyclable products
made from wood grown in sustainable forests. The manufacturing processes
conform to the environmental regulations of the country of origin.

ISBN: 978-1-78929-647-1 in paperback print format
ISBN: 978-1-78929-345-6 in ebook format

1 2 3 4 5 6 7 8 9 10

www.mombooks.com

Cover design by Claire Cater
Cover illustration by Shutterstock
Designed and typeset by Design 23
Illustrations by David Woodroffe

Printed and bound by CPI Group (UK) Ltd, Croydon, CR0 4YY

Contents

PART 4: MENTAL EXERCISE

PART 5: SOCIAL LIFE

PART 6: HEALTHY BODY, HEALTHY MIND

PART 7: THE INFLUENCE OF YOU

Introduction

Just as I was coming to the end of writing this book, I happened to have my first ever appointment with a neurologist. The debilitating migraines that used to afflict me every now and again had become a regular occurrence, and I wanted to get to the bottom of it. Sitting behind an imposing desk, the neurologist asked me various questions about my lifestyle, my family history and my headaches. When I admitted I couldn't put my finger on what specifically triggers the migraines, he told me not to worry: even he – a neurologist with a special training in migraine and headaches – couldn't tell me what causes his own.

By the end of our consultation, reassured that it was probably nothing too sinister, the doctor took out a piece of paper and scribbled down the name of something I could take that had been proven in trials to help some people with migraines. It wasn't a fancy new drug or a strong painkiller – instead, his note read: 'Vitamin B2 (Riboflavin) 400 mg'.

Vitamin B2 is found in foods like almonds, broccoli and eggs, of which I eat plenty, and has many known uses in the body including helping turn food into energy, and proper functioning of the nervous system. We only need a fraction each day of the 400 mg my neurologist prescribed – but several trials have shown that people taking large quantities of the vitamin had fewer migraines and that they became shorter in duration. One study even found it cut the number of migraines in half. As a science journalist, the first thing I did was look up those studies and assess the evidence for myself. I'm still a little sceptical but seeing as there are no side effects (except my urine turning luminous yellow), I'm willing to give it a go. As well as making me feel a little better about my migraines, my neurology appointment also highlighted a lot of important things about the brain I have discovered while writing this book – information useful to us all.

Let's start with the fact that my doctor – one of the top headache specialists around – was actually somewhat in the dark about what causes many headaches. It would be clichéd of me to tell you that the human brain is the most complex object in the known universe, but the fact is it is truly, unbelievably complex, and despite decades of research we are only just starting to scratch the surface of how it works. We don't yet know all the cells that make up the brain, let alone how they communicate with each other to create our complex thoughts, emotions, behaviours, sensations, and – best of all – our sense of consciousness. So I'll forgive my neurologist for not knowing all the details.

You might take from this that we should simply give up. The brain is too complicated for us to make sense of … but that's not right either. We are constantly discovering new information about the workings of the brain, especially with the help of technologies like MRI scans, which allow us to see the brain in action. These are incredibly exciting times in neuroscience, and we can put this new knowledge to good use. However, we just need to remember that science is an ongoing process. In some areas that I cover in this book, especially the powerful influence of exercise, sleep, keeping mentally engaged and having strong social connections, the jury is in – there are definite ways to boost our brain power through our actions. In others, the evidence is less clear cut. But these developing areas of our understanding are fascinating, and certainly worth being aware of as research progresses.

Now let's turn to those B vitamins – and this is where things get exciting. There is today a growing appreciation that the brain does not work in isolation from the body, and that problems of the mind are intricately connected to our physical health. I don't know about you, but if my headaches can be prevented by a vitamin top-up, I'd rather address that than simply take painkillers to treat the symptoms of the migraines (though I will certainly take those drugs when needed). Excitingly, recent studies suggest that the environment, rather than genetics, has the most influence on how the brain changes as we age, and eventual cognitive decline,[1] leaving no doubt that what we choose to do in our daily lives is crucial to our brain health.

This way of thinking is revolutionary because it points to the myriad ways that keeping the body in good health, as well as other hobbies and habits, will also keep our minds firing on all cylinders, and it is these that we discuss in this book.

It also means that we shouldn't wait until things go wrong – until we are sitting in front of that neurologist's desk – to look after our brain health. If anything, this book is a manifesto to take control of your brain health *now*. And the sooner you start the better.

This revolution couldn't come soon enough. By 2030, the number of people aged sixty years or over is predicted to grow by 56 per cent to 1.4 billion.[2] With this ageing population, the likelihood of developing neurodegenerative diseases, such as Alzheimer's disease and vascular dementia, will also skyrocket. And yet half of us would be incapable of listing the risk factors for dementia.[3] Unfortunately, we also still have a sketchy understanding of the causes of Alzheimer's, and treatments have not been forthcoming. That means lifestyle factors that can prevent and slow this disease are more vital than ever.

Throughout this book we talk about things we can do – and things we can avoid – to improve our brain health. But what does it even mean to have a healthy, happy brain? Within these pages, I've taken a healthy brain to mean a brain that is functioning as expected, based on measures such as the structure of the brain, and how well it works when examined in a brain scanner. We'll also talk a lot about how the brain changes with age, and what we can do to keep any detrimental changes, those that tip us towards dementia in particular, to a minimum. As for a happy brain, what we are really talking about here is mood. That encompasses mental-health conditions that affect our mood such as depression and anxiety, as well as other states that can make us feel bad, like stress. We'll also be looking at ways we can all give our mood an instant boost – unrelated to any mood disorders. Within both of these categories, we'll also be talking about cognitive performance – in other words, how to keep our brains sharp, whether that's an immediate burst of attention, focus or creativity, or keeping our wits about us in the long term.

It is worth noting that while this book focuses on the brain almost exclusively, many of the things covered here can be hugely beneficial to the body, too. Even better, many of them are also free, often don't take much time, and can be a lot of fun. So embarking on a journey to improve your brain health will probably improve your life in all sorts of other ways too.

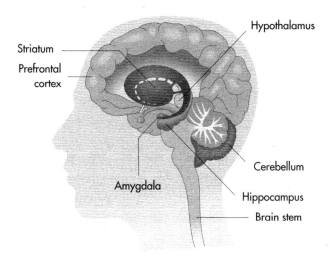

Striatum
Prefrontal cortex
Hypothalamus
Cerebellum
Amygdala
Hippocampus
Brain stem

Ultimately, a healthy brain is about feeling good. My hope is that this book will help you identify changes big or small that you might want to implement in your life, both now and as you age, that do not feel like a chore or a punishment. I would encourage you to try things out and see if they work for you, but if they feel onerous, give them a miss and opt for something else.

Before we start, let's return one last time to that neurologist's office, and his advice to try B vitamins. That compelling clinical trial cut the incidence of migraine in half ... but only for some of the people in the study. For others, it had no effect. Whether I will be one of the people it works for remains to be seen, but it's important to remember that our remarkable brains are what make us unique. Each one is different and there is no one-size-fits-all solution. It would be remiss of me not to point out that many people do, and will, experience mental-health problems and neurological diseases regardless of lifestyle choices. The point here is that our actions can hugely influence our brain health, but we still don't have all the answers.

Similarly, there is no silver bullet. Your best bet for protecting your brain is to take on a combination of the beneficial habits, and let the effects build. This isn't about a quick fix, but about lifestyle changes that last.

Maybe one day in the future, scientists will develop a pill to pop that mimics the effects of brain-healthy habits: that can replace the benefits of exercise, a glass of red wine in the company of good friends, a solid relationship; of walks in nature, a good night's sleep, the feeling of the warming sun on your face and the influence of nutritious food. When that happens, you will be free to gulp down that pill and instantly reap all the benefits, letting you get on with something else. Or, and this is my hope at least, you will discover such enjoyment in the very things that keep your brain healthy and happy, you will want to keep doing them well into your long and healthy life.

PART 1

DIET

The brain is a hungry organ, consuming about 20 per cent of the body's energy. And yet, when we choose what to eat, we are more likely to be thinking about the effects on our physical health. Is it good for the heart? Will it make me put on weight? Does it cause cancer or diabetes? It's not just individuals who think this way: by and large the medical profession too has underappreciated the role that diet plays in our mental wellbeing. That is despite the fact that we have long known that the gut is not a standalone organ, and that it is in constant dialogue with the brain. Now, science is starting to home in on this conversation, and the findings are quite astounding.

One way that the gut and brain communicate is through the microbiome, on which there has been an explosion of research in recent years. In Chapter 1, we get acquainted with the trillions of microbes living within us, and discover the incredible ways they influence our wellbeing. Crucially, we will also learn how to feed them to keep them – and by default, ourselves – happy.

In Chapter 2, we go on to explore the idea that it isn't just what we eat, but also *when*, that plays a role in staying sharp. Fasting diets of all types are growing in popularity, but are they all they are cracked up to be, and can going hungry really fine-tune your brain?

Bad diet is the leading risk factor for death in the majority of countries around the world, claiming more lives than smoking.[4] Where have we gone wrong? In Chapter 3, we take a tour of some of the global hotspots that have the healthiest diets, and learn from them and the latest research about what we should actually be eating for optimal brain health and a long and healthy life.

Finally, if you still aren't convinced about the role of diet on the brain, in Chapter 4 we turn to what happens when our body's ability to cope with food breaks down, and to the striking idea that Alzheimer's disease could be a kind of diabetes of the brain.

Throughout this part of the book, we will discover the antidote to the multitude of diets and fads that promise a quick fix, and instead learn the sustainable, delicious changes that we can make to our diets to keep our brains fighting fit.

CHAPTER 1

What to eat to boost your mood

Butterflies in your stomach on a first date, a gut feeling that someone isn't being honest with you, even a tummy upset in anticipation of a big work presentation: we have all experienced the connection between the gut and the brain in some form. But did you know that the gut has its own nervous system? Or that the gut is in constant dialogue with the brain, influencing your thoughts and moods even when you aren't eating? This connection is so strong that scientists have come to call the gut our second brain, and are gleaning a better understanding than ever of how we can all nurture this connection to feel and think better.

The two-way communication between the gut and the brain is called the gut–brain axis, and information can travel back and forth in a number of ways. The most direct is the vagus nerve, an information super-highway that sends signals from our gut to our central nervous system, and is a key player in the body's 'rest and digest' mode. The vagus nerve is considered to be the body's sixth sense,[5] because of its ability to detect activity in our organs and communicate that important information back to the brain. Aside from the vagus nerve, the gut can talk to the brain in other ways, including through hormones, the immune system and through our gut microbes.

Our understanding of the influence of the gut–brain axis on our mental health is relatively new, especially the role of the microbes that live in our gut. Even so, it's an extremely exciting area of research, with compelling evidence that the way we treat these residents of our intestines can have a profound influence.

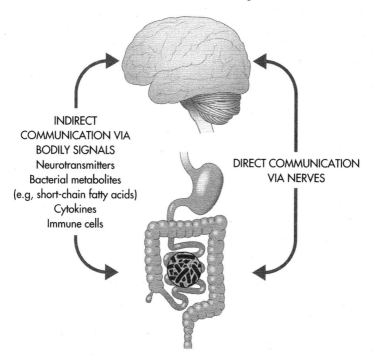

INDIRECT
COMMUNICATION VIA
BODILY SIGNALS
Neurotransmitters
Bacterial metabolites
(e.g, short-chain fatty acids)
Cytokines
Immune cells

DIRECT COMMUNICATION
VIA NERVES

Meet your microbiome

We have an estimated 40 trillion microorganisms living in our digestive tract. To put this into perspective, this is about the same number as cells that make up the human body, and there are 100,000 times more microbes in your gut than there are people on the Earth.[6]

They predominantly make their home in the large intestine, the final part of the digestive tract, and the slowest part of the digestive system, taking about twelve to thirty hours to process what's coming through, giving plenty of time for our gut microbes to work their magic. These trillions of microbes, which include bacteria, viruses, fungi and parasites, are together called our microbiota. In combination they house hundreds of times more genes than your own genome – all the genetic material in your own body. It is this collection of microbial genes that we call the microbiome.

Remarkably, until the twenty-first century, 80 per cent of the microbes in our guts were a mystery to us. That's changing thanks to gene-sequencing technology, and in 2007 the Human Microbiome Project was launched to sequence our 'second genome'. We are now entering an exciting phase, where the focus is shifting from what these inhabitants are, to what they are getting up to in there – and how we can make the most of them to influence our physical and mental health.[7]

We often hear talk of 'good bacteria', and this is a key concept when we think about our gut microbiota. Our digestive tract is one of the prime ways that harmful organisms can enter the body. If we have enough 'good' bacteria in there, any unwanted pathogens will be outnumbered, helping to protect us from infection. This is one reason why, when it comes to health, it's important to have as diverse a microbiome as possible. The more skills it can perform, the more it can do to keep us well.

But our gut-residents do much more than simply outcompete harmful microbes. They also break down foods that are indigestible to us, producing a number of useful compounds, or metabolites, and make vitamins, including all eight B vitamins. Remarkably, our gut microbes can also produce neurotransmitters, the chemicals our brain cells use to communicate, including serotonin (a lack of which is implicated in depression), noradrenaline (which primes the body for action) and dopamine (which plays a vital role in mood, and in our ability to learn and plan). In fact, 50 per cent of our dopamine is made in the gut.[8]

Powerful influencers

All of this goes to show that our gut microbes are not merely passengers hitching a ride inside us. Their health is tightly connected to our own, and they can exert a powerful influence over our brain.

Just how big that influence is has started to become clear through research over the past decade or so, starting with studies in germ-free mice. These are mice that are bred without any microbes and raised in a sterile environment, allowing scientists to see what effect exposure to various microbes has on them. Pioneering research in 2004 by a team of Japanese researchers found that these microbiome-free mice had underdeveloped brains, an exaggerated stress response, and seemed to act as though they were depressed.[9] Tellingly, after the mice were fed a mix of bacteria, their stress response quickly became normal.

Further compelling evidence comes from studies using faecal transplants, during which faecal material from one individual is transferred to the gut of another, often through an enema or sometimes orally, for instance in pill form. One review of this technique, published in 2020, looked at studies of faecal transplants into mice from people with specific conditions. After the mice received the transplant, they developed symptoms similar to those seen in humans – including depression, anxiety, anorexia and alcoholism. Of course, these symptoms aren't exactly the same as in people, but are a proxy – for instance, mice displaying anxiety will spend less time in the middle of an open field, preferring to stick to the edges. Those displaying compulsive behaviours will frantically bury marbles, given the chance. Simply transferring the microbiome of someone who is poorly into these mice seemed to also transfer the health issue.

What if we could do the opposite, and transfer the microbiome of healthy individuals into those with pre-existing health conditions, in an attempt get rid of them? It's a tantalizing idea, and while few studies have taken place in people, a handful do exist. For instance, the review identified six studies where feacal transplants took place from healthy volunteers to people with depression, and all of the studies found short-term improvements in depressive symptoms in those receiving the transplants. However, the symptoms generally returned to previous levels after several months.

ANTIBIOTICS AND THE MICROBIOME

On the whole, antibiotics seem to be bad news for your microbiome, messing with the balance of microbes in your gut (of course they are also an incredibly important treatment for bacterial infections, so you should still follow doctor's orders where needed). However, the picture is complicated by evidence suggesting that activity of antibiotics on the microbiome might also help people with persistent negative symptoms of schizophrenia or those with depression who are resistant to standard treatments. So the role of antibiotics on the microbiome – in both the treatment and prevention of disease – is likely to become a hot topic in the years to come.

As for how these effects take place, it could be through any of the number of ways the gut talks to the brain. Neurotransmitters and short-chain fatty acids, produced when gut microbes chew up fibre from our diet that we can't digest ourselves, can both fire up the vagus nerve, sending signals to the brain. Indeed, when mice have their vagus nerve cut, the beneficial effects of gut microbes disappear.

Short-chain fatty acids are also anti-inflammatory and can influence the immune system in other ways too. Given that many psychiatric illnesses are influenced by inflammation (see Chapter 25 for more on this), the anti-inflammatory powers of the gut microbiome are particularly intriguing.

The psychobiotic revolution

Faecal transplants are still an extreme option and in 2020 the US Food and Drug Administration (FDA) issued a warning over the risk of serious infections related to the practice.[10] An alternative suggestion is that we might give people probiotics – bacteria that have proven health benefits for the gut – as a way to treat mental-health problems, an idea that leading researchers John Cryan and Ted Dinan at University College Cork in Ireland and their colleagues coined 'psychobiotics'.

But how sure can we be that effects of the microbiome we see in animals apply to humans? One piece of evidence starts with a tragedy in 2000 in the Canadian town of Walkerton, Ontario, when heavy rains caused the water supply to become infected with *E. coli* and *campylobacter* from cattle excrement. It resulted in an epidemic of bacterial dysentery, which infected half of the population and tragically killed seven. Many of the survivors went on to develop post-infectious irritable bowel syndrome. But, says Dinan, a significant proportion of patients developed major depressive illness by the end of the first year, suggesting that the pathogen somehow managed to impact on their brains.[11] Research also shows that people with depression, PTSD and schizophrenia have striking similarities in their microbiome that they do not share with matched controls.

Adding to the idea that our gut microbes influence our emotions, investigations of healthy women using brain scans have shown that the levels of certain bacteria in their guts influences the way they respond to emotional pictures – so much so that researchers could use the brain images to predict which kind of gut bacteria the women had. This was pretty convincing evidence that these gut-residents can influence our emotional responses.[12]

The team responsible for these findings, from the University of California, Los Angeles, went on to show that giving women a probiotic yogurt containing bacteria twice a day for four weeks improved the way their brains processed emotions. In clinical populations – that is to say, those already with a mental-health condition – probiotics might also help. In some studies, the approach has been found to reduce symptoms of depression and anxiety.[13]

Before you head off to stock up on probiotic yogurt, hold fire. There are plenty of products on sale that claim all sorts of benefits to our health, but even Dinan says that the majority of probiotics his group have tested in the lab yielded no effect on the mind, and there's no guarantee that the bacteria ingested will survive the journey through your stomach acid to reach the large intestine. To make matters worse, not only are we in the dark about which bacteria are going to be truly effective in boosting mood, but each of us also has a different gut microbiota, so the likelihood is that what works for one will not work for all. Until we figure all this out, the promise of psychobiotics remains just a promise for now.

Take care of your microbes

It seems clear that protecting the trillions of helpful microbes living within our guts and keeping them healthy can also help to protect our mental health.

But how do we best do that? According to the gut-health doctor Megan Rossi, at King's College London, the most important thing is to eat a diverse range of plant-based foods, in order to nurture a diverse microbiome. She says that due to modern agricultural techniques, the diversity of our plant food sources has plummeted, with 75 per cent of the world's food generated from just twelve plant species.[14] So the challenge is on to eat as wide a variety of plants as possible – she recommends at least thirty different plant-based foods a week. This might sound daunting, but with a few tricks up your sleeve (see the box opposite) they add up fast. While you're at it, make sure you include plenty of fibre, which can't be broken down by our digestive systems but feeds our microbiome, and is then split into those all-important short-chain fatty acids that are so good for us. They also seem to help regulate stress and anxiety.[15]

SIMPLE WAYS TO EAT BETTER FOR YOUR MICROBIOME

- Eat mainly plants and try to get in at least thirty different varieties of plant-based foods a week. This includes fruit and vegetables, pulses, nuts and seeds. Fibre, especially wholegrain, is particularly good.
- Avoid too much refined and heavily processed food, and sugary food and drinks.
- Herbs and spices are an easy way to add variety to your diet, and pack it full of flavour too.
- If you have access to a weekly fruit-and-veg-box delivery, it can be a fun way to increase the diversity of the food you normally eat.
- Sprinkle mixed nuts and seeds on top of cereal, yogurt or soup – each variety counts towards your weekly thirty.
- The same goes for mixed salad leaves – an easy way to diversify your diet with minimal effort.
- Freeze excess fruit and vegetables to retain most of the nutrients, and pop them into smoothies or other dishes.

Other than diet, there are several things we can also do to help look after our microbiota. One of those is to get enough sleep. Your gut microbiome has its own circadian rhythm, with its activity following a twenty-four-hour cycle, so disrupted sleep can mess with it too. And getting more sleep helps us to make healthier food decisions – a win-win for the microbiome. (See Part 2 of this book for tips on getting better sleep.)

Stress can make the gut leakier, allowing bacteria into the bloodstream. This can trigger inflammation, too much of which is bad for both physical and mental health. Cryan and his colleagues have done research in mice that shows that the short-chain fatty acids that are released by gut microbes after we eat fibre can help repair some of this damage – another reason to get that fruit and veg into your diet.

All in all, the evidence is mounting that the gut influences our moods and vice versa. When we feed ourselves to feel good, we should consider what our gut microbes like to eat too – keeping them onside is likely to become an increasingly important way to bolster our physical and mental health.

CHAPTER 2

Going hungry could keep your brain young

If you are a diehard breakfast fan, this chapter might be hard to swallow. I'm a firm believer that breakfast tastes so great because we've usually not eaten for a good ten or more hours beforehand. But what if you could hold off a little longer? The impact on your brain might be worth the effort.

Neurogenesis – the growth of new brain cells – has been linked to increased cognition and better mood, but unfortunately it naturally decreases with age. In fact, until relatively recently, the ability to grow new brain cells was considered to be exclusive to the young, with adults stuck with those they acquired in childhood and their teenage years. Happily, evidence is now stacking up that adults too can grow brain cells in some areas, including the hippocampus, well into old age, and as a result, any strategy that gives rise to these new cells is good news (see Chapter 16 for more on neurogenesis). One approach that's garnered a lot of attention is calorie restriction, otherwise known as fasting.

Hungry worms

The practice of fasting has long been a part of religious and cultural traditions, and the scientific community is catching on. All kinds of organisms, from yeast to worms and mice, live longer (as much as 80 per cent longer in the case of rats) when put on a highly calorie-restricted diet, generally one that sees them cutting out around 40 per cent of their daily calories.

Dieting in this way seems to be particularly beneficial for the brain, in other animals at least. Mice that were given a rodent-version of Alzheimer's disease, for instance, and who then ate 30 per cent fewer calories for four months, had improvements in markers of the disease on the brain. As long as vitamins, minerals and other essential nutrients are coming in, mice on a calorie-restricted diet have been found to have increased brain plasticity and better function of synapses, the connections between brain cells that play a vital role in learning and memory.[16] And mice put on a long-term calorie-restricted diet also had improvements in their working memory, which you can think of as the ability to hold numerous pieces of information in your mind while you do something else – a skill that decreases markedly as the brain ages.

Why might eating less be good for us? As our cells break down the food we eat, they release rogue compounds called free radicals that can damage other cells and tissues and contribute to the ageing process. So one theory on the benefits of fasting is that eating less gives our metabolism a break, affording our body respite from this process.

Miserable lifestyle

The potential of calorie restriction as a route to a longer, healthier life has led some determined individuals to give it a go, strictly limiting the amount they eat day in day out. For most us, however, consistently eating so few calories would leave us feeling miserable and hungry, and possibly questioning the appeal of living longer in such a state of mind.

Recently, however, scientists realized there could be a simpler way to achieve the effects of fasting without the perpetual hunger. They noticed that when animals are put on a calorie-restricted diet in experiments, they tend to simply be given their food in a smaller window, and eat nothing at all the rest of the time, rather than being allowed to eat a smaller amount throughout the day. And there is a growing consensus that it is this switching between fasting and eating normally again that makes calorie-controlled diets so good for the body and brain. Indeed, studies looking specifically at intermittent fasting protocols, where animals are allowed to feed during a small allotted time window, have shown promising results, including for obesity, diabetes, cardiovascular disease, cancers and neurodegenerative diseases.

FASTING AND BRAIN DISORDERS

In the next few years, it will be interesting to see whether fasting can help with symptoms of brain disorders such as Alzheimer's disease, Parkinson's and stroke. Animal studies certainly look promising, not least because ketones that are produced when we fast and used by the body for fuel have been shown to stimulate the production of a molecule called BDNF, which is important for learning and memory, and the ability of the brain to adapt to stress, as well as in helping the brain to protect itself against disease. Furthermore, fasting rodents that have Alzheimer's-like brains do better on learning and memory tasks. Fasting has even been shown to reduce damage in the brains of animals that have been given something akin to a stroke. One of the reasons ketones might be a promising area of examination for Alzheimer's disease is that the brains of people with the disorder have a reduced ability to use glucose, possibly because the transport of glucose is blocked by amyloid plaques that build up in the brains of people with Alzheimer's. So, switching to a different energy source could be beneficial to maintaining brain function.

The thinking is now that, rather than passively reducing free radicals produced from digestion, intermittent fasting puts the body into a kind of repair mode, where it becomes better at mopping up bits of debris and triggering pathways that actively protect the body against free radicals. Fasting makes the cells in the body and brain better able to cope with stress, and has been found to improve immune function, as well as memory, learning, cognitive skills and alertness.[17] For mice, intermittent fasting also reverses the cognitive impairment associated with obesity and diabetes. In other words, the minor physical stress imposed by a relatively short period of fasting seems to transform the body and brain into more efficient machines. And when feeding resumes, it triggers a flurry of growth and new connections in the brain. It's a bit like weeding and pruning a garden to allow new shoots and stronger branches to grow.

Ketosis boost

That's not all. After some time without food, the body will have burned through all the glucose circulating in the blood, and the glycogen stored in the liver. At this point it will have run out of sugars to use as fuel and will need to find a new energy source. And so, it begins converting stored fat into ketone bodies, another type of fuel that the body and brain can use for energy instead of sugars. This process, called ketosis, is thought to underpin many of the possible beneficial effects associated with fasting, and is the concept behind the popular ketogenic diet, where people eat next to no sugars and other carbohydrates, so the body burns fat stores instead. Ketones have been shown in animal studies to trigger numerous health-promoting processes, including the production of BDNF (a molecule that plays an important part in learning and memory) – which might explain the anecdotal reports that people feel mentally sharper when they fast – and trials are underway to see whether the same thing happens in humans too.

Helpful hunger

The idea of going hungry to help the mind function better can feel counterintuitive. Food is fuel, after all, and it can be hard to get much done on an empty stomach. But the benefits of fasting make sense if we think about animals in the wild, which wouldn't be guaranteed a continuous food source and instead would likely go through periods of fast and famine. It would be no good if that hunger left them moping around feeling sorry for themselves. On the contrary, when food was scarce, they'd need to be especially cognitively sharp in order to hunt down their next meal, or remember a previous food source.

The million-dollar question is whether the same is true in humans. In evolutionary terms, there's no reason why it shouldn't be. Although many of us have the luxury of 24/7 convenience stores, online shopping and fast-food delivery, long periods of food scarcity would have been more common for our ancestors. This cycle of fast and famine may even have contributed to the complexity of the human brain, with the pressure of food scarcity forcing its evolution, says Mark Mattson who studies fasting at Johns Hopkins University. Tellingly, he points out, domesticated dogs that have abundant and constant access to food have smaller brains than wild dogs – suggesting that plentiful food could be shrinking their brains.[18]

All this has led to an explosion in the popularity of a plethora of fasting diets, which each involve a period of time with no, or very little food intake, followed by normal eating. You've probably heard of many of these: the 5:2 diet involves eating normally for five days a week and severely restricting calorie intake the other two; the 8:16 diet has you eating during an eight-hour window; the OMAD diet (or one meal a day) restricts food to just one hour; and alternate-day fasting is self-explanatory.

TIPS FOR GIVING FASTING A GO

1. Fasting makes a lot of people feel irritable, hungry and unable to concentrate, but these effects do tend to pass after you've been practising for about a month, so don't give up too soon.

2. Fast-track the effects with exercise. Many of the benefits of fasting are thought to come from switching from burning carbohydrates to burning fats. It should take at least ten hours to burn through the carb stores in your liver and blood, but you can give the process a boost with exercise. An hour-long run before breakfast, for instance, gets your body to switch to fat-burning mode.

3. Ease into it. Try eating your first meal of the day an hour later, and your last meal an hour earlier, then tighten that window once you've adjusted.

4. Don't be too extreme. Fasting diets are thought to be beneficial to the body and brain because they involve a period of restraint followed by normal eating in which the body has a period of growth, so don't be tempted to fast for too long without the normal feeding period.

Studies of the effects of fasting diets on the human brain are, however, harder to come by than those in other animals. Plus, people haven't been eating this way for long enough for us to see the long-term effects properly. There are, though, some encouraging signs. One study of people over seventy found that they had a dramatic improvement in verbal memory (the ability to remember what you read or hear) after three months of intermittent fasting.[19] Another study of people who were obese and had mild cognitive impairment, a risk factor for Alzheimer's disease, had improvements in memory, cognition and executive function after twelve months of calorie restriction. And in 2020, Dr Sandrine Thuret at King's College London and her colleagues found that calorie restriction improved a type of memory linked to the growth of new brain cells in the hippocampus.[20]

Fasting scientists

Even if the jury is still out, anecdotally, scientists who study fasting practise what they preach, so they obviously think there's something in it. Thuret once told me she follows a fasting pattern in which she eats every other day (on fasting days she still eats, opting for something like a latte, fruit and a cereal bar). Mattson champions a 6:18-style diet, where he eats all his food within a six-hour window, and tends to also do a good bout of exercise towards the end of his fast to double down on ketosis.[21]

It's worth bearing in mind, however, that many of the studies, both in other animals and humans, have been done on overweight individuals or those with other health issues. If you are already young and healthy, fasting may have less of an effect. Tantalizing as the evidence is, we don't quite know whether the benefits we see in animals truly do extend to humans. And if you're tempted to give fasting a go, remember that it isn't suitable for some people, including those who are pregnant, or who already have a problematic relationship with food, so you should talk to your doctor before embarking on a new diet. As we will find later on in the book in relation to exercise, genes can also play a part in how the body responds to lifestyle approaches to brain health: it is possible that fasting works well for the brain of someone with a certain set of genes, but might also do nothing – or even be harmful – in those with other genetic variants.

However, some of the habits that fasting brings – like making us more aware of what we are eating, and not snacking late into the evening – can be beneficial more generally, not least because our digestive system has its own circadian rhythm and works better earlier on in the day. Besides, waiting a few hours might just make your breakfast taste even more delicious.

CHAPTER 3

The promise of brain-boosting foods

Blueberries to boost your memory. Eggs to stop your brain shrinking. Sage to help you concentrate. The internet – and let's not get started on the aisles of health-food shops – is bursting with information about so-called brain-boosting foods. But is any of it true?

The first thing to say is that it's incredibly difficult to find out the answers to this question. Really good-quality research into the effects of diet on our health is hard to do. That's in part because we don't eat single nutrients, we eat foods in combination with other foods, preserved, cooked and consumed in various ways. Teasing out the effect of blueberries, say, from the other things we eat is practically impossible. Besides, we might also want to ask whether people eat their blueberries in a smoothie or in a pie with ice cream, fresh versus frozen, or whether they only eat them in season. Foods interact with each other in different ways too. One good example is that vitamin C helps with the absorption of iron. So let's imagine blueberries make people feel less tired. The benefits might not be due to the blueberries themselves, but due to the increased iron absorption. Perhaps another fruit rich in vitamin C would be just as good.

Food diary fraud

Another issue is that we can't always easily separate out diet from other lifestyle factors. Blueberries are expensive. Perhaps people who eat more of them also have more money, and leisure time for piano lessons and Pilates, which could be benefiting their brains. Finally, if we want to understand the effect of diet on health in the long term, we can't realistically ask a big group of people to start eating blueberries once a week from six months of age and compare their brains aged sixty. Instead, many studies rely on asking people what they have eaten in the past and, sadly, we are notoriously bad at answering this accurately – whether because we consciously massage the truth or unintentionally omit certain details. All of which is to say that much of the literature out there should be taken with a very generous pinch of salt.

With the warning out of the way, let's turn to what we do know. If we want to go straight to the horse's mouth to find out what we need to do for a long and healthy life, there are five places around the world that have the highest concentrations of centenarians – people who have made it to 100 years old or more. These top locations known as blue zones (in case you're wondering, so named because of the colour pen originally used by researchers to mark up their map), span the globe from the Nicoya Peninsula in Costa Rica to Okinawa in Japan and Sardinia in Italy (see the map on page 32). These places have many commonalities that could explain why people there live so long – including a love for physical activity and a strong focus on social connection and a sense of purpose.

As for diet, what these populations eat varies from place to place, but one common feature is that their diets are heavily plant-based. Some do eat meat, but in small quantities. Eggs and dairy are also, by and large, consumed in moderation. They generally eat whole foods rather than heavily processed junk food, and drink little alcohol – and the booze they do drink is

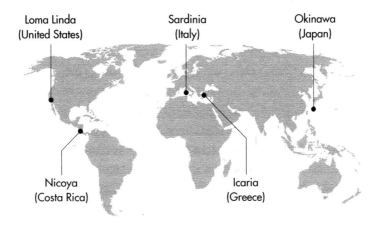

Loma Linda (United States) Sardinia (Italy) Okinawa (Japan)

Nicoya (Costa Rica) Icaria (Greece)

mainly wine. Two out of five of these blue zones also follow the Mediterranean diet, which is renowned for its health effects.

The idea of eating lots of plants fits with what we know about the microbiome, and indeed some recent research suggests that the very reason the Mediterranean diet is so good for us is the way it influences our gut microbes.[22] People in Okinawa also tend to eat very few calories, even by Japanese standards, a hint that keeping calories low, as we learned in the previous chapter, could be a good strategy for health. The diets of blue-zoners also fits with the recent finding that a poor diet is the leading cause of death in most countries. The biggest culprits? Too much salt, too few whole grains and not enough vegetables. Exactly the opposite of the blue-zone diet.

Med diet marvel

Living longer is one thing, but what about the brain? Here, the Mediterranean diet really comes into its own. Studies consistently find that sticking to it reduces the risk for numerous brain conditions including stroke, depression and Alzheimer's.[23] On the other hand, unhealthy diets high in processed foods have been linked to increased risk of depression as well as anxiety.[24]

Diet and mental health, then, are clearly connected, but most of these studies are observational – meaning that people's habits are observed and measurements are made, but the scientists aren't trying to change the outcome – so we can't definitively say that diet is the driving force.

That's starting to change. Our growing understanding of the role of diet in mental health has led to the emergence of a field of research called nutritional psychiatry, which puts to the test the exciting prospect that diet could be a tool to prevent and, crucially, treat mental illness. Nutritional psychiatrists want to see whether we could use diet to alleviate some of the symptoms of mental illness, and this is where things get really interesting.

One of the first such intervention trials happened by mistake. The researchers wanted to know whether a kind of psychotherapy could help people with early depressive symptoms, who are likely to go on to develop full-blown depression. Because they weren't aware of the role of diet in mental health, as it was still a very new area of research, the researchers decided to use nutritional advice instead of psychotherapy for the control group, assuming this would have no effect on depression. They were surprised to discover that those people who received psychotherapy and those who had the dietary advice saw the same reduction in their chances of going on to develop depression – around 8 per cent rather than 20–25 per cent for those who receive neither.[25]

That was the first indication that diet could help with the symptoms of depression. Then, in 2017, came the SMILES trial[26] (which stands for Supporting the Modification of lifestyle In Lowered Emotional States) led by nutritional psychiatrist Felice Jacka at Deakin University in Australia. This was the first randomized controlled trial looking at whether changing someone's diet could help alleviate their symptoms of depression. Sixty-seven people with depression – who also had an unhealthy diet high in sweets, salty snacks and processed meat, and low

---

SMILES TRIAL – WHAT THEY ATE

The primary focus of this trial was on increasing diet quality by supporting the consumption of the following key food groups (recommended servings in parentheses):

- wholegrains (5–8 servings per day)
- vegetables (6 per day)
- fruit (3 per day)
- legumes (3–4 per week)
- low-fat and unsweetened dairy foods (2–3 per day)
- raw and unsalted nuts (1 per day)
- fish (at least 2 per week)
- lean red meats (3–4 per week)
- chicken (2–3 per week)
- eggs (up to 6 per week)
- olive oil (3 tablespoons per day)

At the same time, participants were told to reduce intake of 'extras' foods, such as sweets, refined cereals, fried food, fast food, processed meats and sugary drinks (no more than three per week). Red or white wine consumption beyond two standard drinks per day and all other alcohol were included within the 'extras'. Individuals were advised to select red wine preferably and only drink with meals.

---

in fruit and vegetables, fibre and lean meat – were signed up. Over the course of twelve weeks they were assigned to either a nutritional intervention, where they were told to follow a diet similar to the Mediterranean diet and received seven hour-long sessions with a nutritionist, or they were assigned to a social support control group. By the end of the study, those who were in the nutrition group were four times as likely to be in remission for depression than those in the control group, and had significantly fewer anxiety symptoms. Excitingly, the diet intervention was more effective than standard treatments of depression.[27]

The findings have since been backed up. In 2019, another similar study in Australia looking at young adults with depression and bad diets found much the same thing.[28] And in 2020, a review of sixteen randomized controlled trials looking at dietary interventions for depression and anxiety, totalling over 45,000 participants, found that depressive symptoms were significantly reduced, with the biggest effects for females. So the evidence is building to show that diet could be a very useful treatment for some people with depression.

Whole-body approach

These studies don't tell us what's actually going on in the body to help with the symptoms, but the researchers think it is probably to do with the gut microbiome, as well as helping to reduce inflammation, which is implicated in many mental-health issues. Importantly, these results show that we need to look at the whole person when we think about brain health and, in particular, treating mental-health conditions – not just the brain itself.

What about those of us who don't have depression, but who nonetheless want to eat well for brain health? Are blueberries, sage and their ilk really the answer? We do know that specific nutrients have a role in optimal brain functioning. For instance, the Mediterranean diet is rich in foods that contain the essential amino acid tryptophan, which the body cannot make by itself and must obtain from food, and is important for production of the feel-good brain chemical serotonin. A varied diet, which contains a lot of fruit and vegetables, will also contain the vitamins and minerals, in particular the B vitamins and vitamin E, that are important for good brain health.

Having said that, we don't eat nutrients, we eat food and meals, so it's not worth fixating too intensely on specific nutrients out of context. Nonetheless, it can still be useful to look at some of the most influential and important nutrients for brain functioning, to make sure we are getting enough. I would also note that whole books could – and have – been written on the subject of diet and the brain, so in this chapter we will take a look at just some of the most common you've probably heard of and may be curious about: essential fats, and polyphenols.

THE OPTIMAL BRAIN DIET?

If you're after the gold-standard brain diet, you might want to check out the MIND diet. This is a tweaked version of the Mediterranean diet, devised by the late Martha Morris, at Rush University Medical Center in Chicago, and is specifically tailored to benefit the brain. Morris ran a trial of over nine hundred people living in retirement homes and assigned them to either the MIND diet, the Mediterranean diet or the DASH diet, which is designed for heart health. Those who stuck to her diet the most strictly had the best Alzheimer's outcomes, slashing their risk of the disease by more than half. The MIND diet advocates you chow down on blueberries and strawberries and sip red wine, but all three diets are quite similar and echo the same advice: eat lots of plants, good fats and oils, and not too much animal fat and processed foods.

Essential fats

The brain is around 11 per cent fat, but it doesn't store fat like the rest of our body does. If it did, in times of food scarcity the brain might start to eat itself, which certainly wouldn't have helped our ancestors' chances of finding their next meal. Instead, the fat in the brain is structural fat, which means it is there not as a store but because it plays a role in the functioning of the brain, being found most abundantly in the fatty sheaths called myelin that insulate many neurons, helping signals to travel faster along them, and making up the brain's white matter.

In spite of this important role for fat, you don't need to be ordering cheeseburgers and chips to feed your brain: the organ can make most of the fats it needs on its own. The big exception is a type of fat called polyunsaturated fatty acids, or PUFAs. These, we need to get from our diet, and two of them in particular are essential for effective brain cell communication, as well as immune function, because they both impact our inflammatory response (albeit in different ways). These are omega-3s and omega-6s. Omega-3s reduce inflammation, and omega-6s promote it, and studies show that we need to eat them in a ratio of 1:2 (one omega-3 for two omega-6s) for optimal brain health. While we need to eat some omega-6s, on a Western diet, we tend to massively over-consume them compared to the omega-3s. When you see which foods they come from, you'll probably understand why.

Foods rich in omega-6s include fat from meats (think pork belly, chicken fat and bacon). Omega-3s can be split into three different types, which come from different sources. Alpha-linoleic acid (ALA) comes from plant sources including flax, hemp and chia seeds and walnuts. Docosahexaenoic acid (DHA) and eicosapentaenoic acid (EPA) come from oily fish, salmon roe and caviar.

If you want to eat one thing to help reduce your risk of dementia, and keep your brain sharp as you age, it's omega-3s. Not only has research shown that older people who consume low amounts of these are 70 per cent more likely to develop dementia than those who consume more, but skimping on these fats could age your brain faster, causing more of the shrinkage in the hippocampus that we see with age. Eating omega-3s can help improve your mood, too. Overall, the studies conclude that at least 4 grams of omega-3s every day will do the job.[29] In her book *Brain Food*, neuroscientist Lisa Mosconi points out that there are simple ways to switch omega-6s for the beneficial omega-3s (in fact, for those wishing to delve deeper into how to eat better for the brain, I recommend picking up her book). My favourite suggestion is to use nut butters such as almond as an alternative to peanut butter, which is high in omega-6.

TIPS FOR A BRAIN-HEALTHY DIET

1. Drink more. The brain needs water for everything it does, but most of us drink too little, and dehydration shrinks the brain. Aim for eight glasses a day to keep your brain hydrated.
2. Combine good diet with exercise. A study of the DASH diet, which is similar to the Mediterranean diet in that it is high in fruit, veg and wholegrain and low in sugar and fat, found that people who followed the regime and also exercised for thirty minutes three times a week saw a 30 per cent boost in cognitive tests after twelve weeks. Another study of the diet in older people with cognitive impairment found that those who also exercised had improvements in executive functions equivalent to a brain eight years younger.
3. Be wary of supplements, especially those touting antioxidant properties. These can sometimes be worse for our health, possibly because they signal to our body to halt its own antioxidant efforts. If in doubt, talk to a doctor.
4. Opt for iodized salt. Iodine deficiency is a major cause of preventable brain damage, and people deficient in the mineral may forfeit fifteen IQ points, according to the World Health Organization.

Polyphenols

Headlines abound about the mood-boosting benefits of chocolate and red wine, but do these do more than just tickle our taste buds? What the two have in common (as well as being delicious), along with fruit and vegetables, spices, tea and coffee, is that they contain nutrients called polyphenols. These are known to be strong antioxidants, meaning they can help mop up dangerous free radicals, and it seems they could improve our mood too. On the whole we can't digest polyphenols, so they end up as food for our gut microbiota, which turn them into other compounds that might be responsible for these effects.

A class of polyphenols called flavonoids that are present in berries, cocoa and spices are of particular interest. Recent research has found that women who eat a lot of these are at lower risk of depression.[30] Another study, over ten years, found that a diet high in flavonoids seemed to slow down cognitive decline in a group of older French adults.[31] What are the best sources? A study looking at the foods most packed with polyphenols found that, per serving, berries, dark chocolate and coffee were all near the top of the charts. Spices too, especially cloves and star anise, are a good bet.

Seeking out some of these ingredients for your recipes might be a smart move, and certainly these findings offer a good excuse to enjoy a square of dark chocolate or the odd glass of wine.

In general, though, based on all the evidence so far, nutritional psychiatrists from the Food and Mood Centre at Deakin University, of which Professor Jacka is director, recommend that the main constituents of our diets should be plant-based foods, including plenty of fruit and veg, as well as salads, legumes (such as chickpeas, lentils and tofu), wholegrains and raw nuts. Fibre is especially important for the gut microbiome and you should aim for 50 grams per day. You should also eat some fish and lean red meat (unless you are vegetarian of course) and healthy fats such as olive oil. Heavily processed foods – the kinds that include lots of fats, salts, sugars and refined carbs – as well as sweeteners and emulsifiers, should be avoided.[32]

You might recognize this diet as standard sensible advice of the type you'd expect to get for a healthy heart, and indeed it is. While that might not sound very exciting, it's good news – what's good for your brain is good for the rest of your body, too.

CHAPTER 4

Alzheimer's could be the diabetes of the brain

You've probably heard of type 1 diabetes, and almost certainly type 2. But what about type 3 diabetes? If you haven't, you might be surprised to know that it is actually referring to Alzheimer's disease.

Type 2 diabetes is a common condition where your body's ability to use and store glucose, or sugar, as a fuel is disrupted. When we eat sugar, the pancreas releases a hormone called insulin, telling liver, muscle and fat cells to turn it into energy. In type 2 diabetes, which is often (but not always) caused by high intake of fatty and sugary foods, and is the most common type of diabetes, this system becomes desensitized and stops working properly, causing blood sugar levels to spike. This type of diabetes is closely linked to obesity and can also result in problems with memory and cognition. What's more, type 2 diabetes is a leading risk factor for Alzheimer's disease.

It's only recently, however, that scientists have discovered an important role for insulin in the brain too. We now know it has two key roles: influencing how much food we eat, and regulating brain signalling and cognitive functions. When insulin can't get into the hippocampus, for instance, this hampers the ability of this part of the brain to form new memories.

It makes sense that a rush of calories – and subsequently insulin – should trigger learning and memory, because it would have helped our ancestors to remember where the best food sources were. But with an abundant diet rich in calories, the process goes awry. The brain can't constantly stay ramped up by sweet treats, and will eventually become immune to these incessant insulin signals.

Diabetes of the mind

This idea that the brain becomes desensitized to insulin during diabetes, causing the associated memory problems, has led some scientists to argue that dementia might in fact be a metabolic disorder. Some of the most compelling evidence on this front comes from the lab of Suzanne de la Monte at Brown University in Providence, Rhode Island.

First, she discovered that in Alzheimer's disease, the hippocampus becomes insensitive to insulin. And when she fed rodents a diet designed to give them type 2 diabetes, they developed the amyloid plaques in the brain that are a tell-tale sign of Alzheimer's. Together, these findings suggest that Alzheimer's could be a kind of diabetes of the brain, which has led some researchers to call it type 3 diabetes – although the name remains controversial.

If the idea is correct, it implies that our addiction to junk food isn't just damaging our bodies, it's also poisoning our minds. But that's only the half of it. It was originally thought that the cognitive decline seen with diabetes was because insulin signalling is important in brain function, so that when areas of the brain become resistant to it, they no longer work properly. The amyloid build-up was seen as an unfortunate by-product of this situation.

However, there are now hints that the amyloid plaques themselves could be the root cause of the dementia people can experience with type 2 diabetes. Precursors to amyloid plaques, small clumps of amyloid called oligomers have been found to block insulin signalling to the hippocampus. The brain does produce enzymes that can get rid of these pesky clumps, but unfortunately these are the same enzymes that are responsible for regulating levels of insulin.[33] When diabetes causes insulin levels to spike, these enzymes exert all their efforts trying to get rid of the insulin, allowing the oligomers to clump together into proper amyloid plaques – further blocking insulin receptors and causing a vicious cycle.

Taken together, these findings have led to the claim that the cognitive decline seen in diabetes might actually be an early form of Alzheimer's. The prevalence of type 2 diabetes is on the rise, with over 570 million people expected to have it by 2025.[34] Worryingly, the suggestion that it could be an early form of Alzheimer's has led many researchers to suspect that the explosion of type 2 diabetes will be followed by a similar dementia trend.

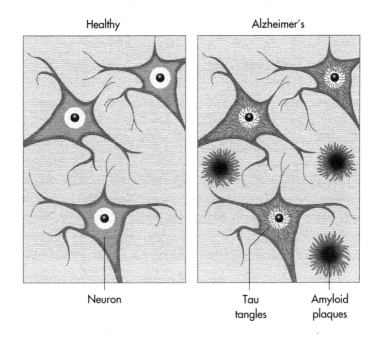

Healthy   Alzheimer's

Neuron   Tau tangles   Amyloid plaques

The good news

This might sound a terrifying prospect, especially to anyone who already has this kind of diabetes, but if Alzheimer's is truly a diabetes of the brain, it might help us find new ways to treat it. For instance, some early research showing promise suggests insulin delivered to the nose may relieve some memory problems.[35] Other experiments in diabetic rats used special antibodies to block the action of oligomers, and found that the memory problems associated with diabetes were reversed. The hunt is now on to find drugs that might do the same thing but be safe for use in humans. Diabetes medications that are already used to target the insulin imbalance might also help, and one such medication was recently found to reduce symptoms of Parkinson's disease,[36] another condition in which insulin resistance is increasingly being implicated. In 2021, a review of the research found that people with type 2 diabetes have a 21 per cent greater chance of developing Parkinson's and have faster symptom progression.[37]

The scientific community is still divided on the issue, and many believe that there simply isn't enough evidence to call Alzheimer's disease type 3 diabetes. Even proponents of the idea concede that insulin disruption in the brain is likely to be one of many causes of the plaque build-up we see so often, especially as not everyone with Alzheimer's has diabetes. What's more, there are still many questions around the role that these plaques play in the symptoms of the disease, because drugs that target them have been so poor at treating the cognitive symptoms.

Even so, the connection between diabetes and Alzheimer's is possibly the best example of the undeniable link between diet and brain health. When we are tempted to reach for fast-food options, we should think not just about our body but also about our brain. If there was ever an incentive to try and give diabetes-triggering foods a miss, the link to Alzheimer's should be it.

ARE YOU AT RISK OF DIABETES?

We don't fully understand why some people develop diabetes, and some risk factors linked to genetics and ethnicity are out of our control. However, there are things you can do to reduce the risks:

- Keep weight gain in check – the more fat you have, the more easily your cells become resistant to insulin. For people who are pre-diabetic, the American Diabetes Association recommends losing 7–10 per cent of body weight, but this should be part of a conversation with your doctor.
- Drink wisely – avoid sugary drinks, including sugar-loaded tea and coffee as well as fruit juices and smoothies, which contain lots of free sugar. Too much alcohol is also a risk.
- Stay active – exercise helps with weight control, uses glucose, and boosts insulin sensitivity, all of which reduce diabetes risk.
- Eat plenty of fibre-rich foods – these are more filling, and are also thought to help slow the absorption of sugars.
- Cut down on salt, which increases your risk of high blood pressure, which in turn increases the risk of type 2 diabetes.

There are also some risk factors we can't change, but being aware of them is important:

- Family history of diabetes.
- Ethnicity – Black, Hispanic, Native American and Asian people are at greater risk.
- Age – type 2 diabetes is not restricted to adults, but it does become more common as you get older.
- Polycystic ovarian syndrome in women, possibly because of the role insulin resistance plays in causing this syndrome as well as diabetes, although the link is still poorly understood.

PART 2

SLEEP

Sleep is one of the most paradoxical things we do. If we think about it in evolutionary terms, it doesn't seem to make sense for animals, including humans, to switch off our conscious awareness on a daily basis, turning us into sitting ducks for prowling predators. And yet all animals do it. We humans spend a third of our lives sleeping. So you'd expect sleep to have an obvious purpose, something so absolutely vital that it outweighs the deadly risks.

And yet we are still far from understanding the purpose of sleep. Fortunately, research has given us plenty of ideas about why we do it, several of which are discussed in the following chapters. One clear and important role of the sleeping brain is to help us lay down new memories and connect them up to those we already have (see Chapter 5). Without memory there would be no learning, and it is arguably in part the ability to learn that has got us where we are today as a species, so perhaps this is the trade-off for the vulnerability that comes with sleep.

Technologies that allow us to study the sleeping brain have also shed light on exactly what happens inside our heads during those unconscious hours, and a mountain of evidence is revealing just how important it is for mental health and for keeping our brains in shape as we age. For instance, sleep seems to be an important piece of the Alzheimer's puzzle, as we discover in Chapter 6 – an exciting idea that could lead to new ways to detect, prevent and even treat the disease.

Some elements of sleep – most notably dreaming, another mysterious element of our state of slumber – also seem to play an important role in processing our emotions, with important consequences if we don't get enough.

And whatever the true purpose of sleep, we all know from experience how terrible a bad night can make us feel. Not getting enough shut-eye, or sleeping at the wrong times, can be dangerously detrimental to our cognitive function, as we explore in Chapter 7, and impacts on our mental health, as we see in Chapter 8.

In this book we are focusing on the cognitive and mental-health effects of sleep, but sleep disruption has been linked to all manner of health problems, from type 2 diabetes to gastrointestinal disorders and even cancer. So if the mental benefits of a good night's slumber compel you to change your habits, there will also be some important knock-on effects for the rest of your body.

In Chapter 9 we take a look at how much sleep you really need, and the chances are you could do with more. Some sleep researchers believe we are getting less sleep than we have in years, and surveys around the world show that vast numbers of us are not hitting the recommended amount of sleep each day. In a society geared towards productivity, sleep has come to be seen as something that gets in the way of accomplishing our goals. In reality, it would be foolish to think we can achieve anything to the best of our abilities without first valuing our sleep.

CHAPTER 5

Sleeping on it improves learning and memory

When I was growing up, my mother used to tell me that putting my revision notes under my pillow the night before an exam would help me remember more the next day. I optimistically imagined the facts floating up into my brain as if by osmosis. That was wishful thinking, of course, but it turns out my mother was on to something – by making sure I got a good night's sleep before an exam, rather than cramming all night, I was almost certainly helping that information become cemented in my brain, setting me up for success the next day.

While we still don't know exactly why we sleep, what is clear is that the sleeping brain is far from a resting brain. By monitoring what happens inside people's heads while they slumber using a technique called electroencephalography (EEG), in which small sensors are placed over the scalp, we can see that the brain cycles through different kinds of activity during the night. And one prominent idea is that at least some of this activity is the brain busily sorting through the events of the day, and moving some of our experiences into longer-term memory storage.

Before we get on to how to use the memory-boosting effects of sleep to our advantage, we need to understand what happens to the brain in a normal night's sleep. There are two main types of sleep: rapid-eye movement (REM) and non-REM (NREM) sleep. After dropping off at night, we cycle through both of these every ninety minutes or so, and depending on how long you sleep for, you'll get about four or five of these cycles in a typical night's sleep.

Sleep cycles

REM and NREM sleep are not evenly distributed throughout the night (see the diagram opposite). In the first part of the night, just after we fall asleep, our brain has a hunger for NREM sleep, which includes deep, restorative slow-wave sleep. As the night progresses, each sleep cycle contains less of this type and more REM sleep, commonly referred to as 'dream sleep' or 'paradoxical sleep' – because, if you look at the brain during REM sleep, it looks much like it does when we are awake.

REM sleep is so called because of the characteristic eye movements people make when in this sleep phase, and it's also commonly believed to be when we dream. This isn't entirely true, however – while most of our time in REM sleep is indeed spent dreaming, and those dreams tend to be our most vivid and bizarre, we can also dream in NREM sleep, even if the dreams are a lot more dreary. Another hallmark of REM sleep is that our muscles become inactivated, presumably to stop us acting out our dreams.

By comparison, NREM sleep is a lot calmer. Our breathing becomes slower and more regular, and our brain activity slows down. This kind of sleep is thought to be particularly restorative, and when people are sleep deprived, they will have much more NREM sleep when they do nod off again – as if the brain has made it its top priority to catch up on what has been missed.

In the later stages of the NREM part of the sleep cycle we go into our deepest sleep, and our brain waves slow down further. And it is this restorative, slow-wave, non-REM sleep that is thought to be especially important for memory storage, and therefore not something you want to be missing out on the night before a big test.

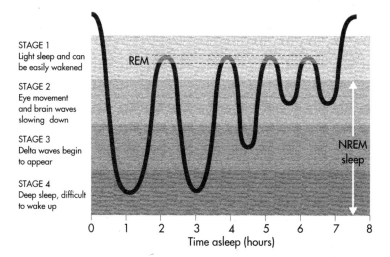

STAGE 1
Light sleep and can
be easily wakened

STAGE 2
Eye movement
and brain waves
slowing down

STAGE 3
Delta waves begin
to appear

STAGE 4
Deep sleep, difficult
to wake up

REM

NREM
sleep

0   1   2   3   4   5   6   7   8
Time asleep (hours)

How memories are made

When we have new experiences or learn novel bits of
information, the brain encodes them as memories, primarily in
the hippocampus. You can think of this memory as a sequence
of brain cells that fire one after the other in a specific pattern
that represents the new bit of information. Just like practising a
skill, every time we trigger this sequence, it becomes reactivated
– strengthening the memory – until eventually it gets moved into
long-term storage. This is the case when we revise for an exam,
repeatedly going over the same material, and reactivating the
memory of the information we want to learn. But it also happens
passively when we snooze: it is now believed that during slow-wave
sleep we reactivate the new memories in the hippocampus, until
they are eventually shunted into the neocortex, an area of the
brain important for complex thought as well as memory, where
they are filed away into long-term storage. You could think of
this process of memory consolidation as a bit like clearing a USB,
moving the files onto your computer and making more space,
says neuroscientist Professor Matthew Walker at the University

of California, Berkeley. With the memories successfully moved to the neocortex, ready for retrieval later on, space is freed up in the hippocampus for new memories to be formed the next day.

Sure enough, when we lack this kind of deep sleep, we have trouble hanging on to memories. Those who suffer from insomnia, for instance, tend to have less slow-wave sleep, and also have impaired memory consolidation. This is also true of general ageing – both slow-wave sleep and memory consolidation decrease after the age of thirty.

Just as missing out on sleep hampers memory performance, getting good sleep helps. Study after study has shown that people perform better in recall tests when they sleep after learning something new, whether it's a proper night's sleep or just a nap. And using brain-stimulation techniques to enhance this kind of slow-wave sleep causes people to remember more the next day. Not all memories, however, are squirrelled away in slow-wave sleep. It is specifically working on declarative memory – our memory for facts and events.

As well as moving our memories into longer-term storage, we now have a growing sense that slow-wave sleep could be strengthening certain memories by 'pruning' the connections in the brain – sorting and reducing the number of connections and leaving only the important circuits. This would help us remember only the most important bits of new information. You could think of this like sculpting a statue out of clay, says Walker, keeping the most important features and cutting away what you don't need.

Brain scans have also revealed bursts of activity during NREM sleep called spindles, which further refine our memories, as if polishing that sculpture.

WHAT IS A MEMORY?

What's the earliest birthday you can remember? It's likely to be some point in your early childhood – so how did that memory get stuck in your brain for you to retrieve today? It doesn't happen all at once. The first step of the journey is called encoding. A representation of that experience gets laid down in the brain. But for that initial memory to persist, it will need what's called consolidation – and lots of it. Every time we rehearse or retrieve a memory it gets reinforced, and sleep seems to play an important part in the process too, reactivating memories and moving them into longer-term storage. Consolidation of memories will make them more resistant to decay over time. While we sleep, the brain also builds networks between different memories so that when we remember one thing it can trigger associated recollections. We don't really understand how the brain chooses which experiences to store away and which to ignore, but emotion is an important component (see Chapter 8), and it gives priority to negative emotions in particular, which could be advantageous from an evolutionary perspective. Sleep also prioritizes things that we believe to be important, for instance information we know we are going to get tested on the next day.

Sleep after learning

If you've ever woken up with a fresh idea or a solution to a problem you went to bed with, this too is thanks to your sleeping brain giving you a creativity boost.

So my mother's instinct about getting a solid night's sleep before an exam was spot on – it could help you consolidate those memories or allow you a burst of creativity, even if you don't literally need to sleep on your revision as I did. But there's more – if you really want to boost your chances of learning something new, you should aim to sleep not only after you revise, but beforehand too.

HOW TO NAP FOR SUCCESS

Forget the idea that napping is lazy – a strategic daytime snooze can reap many a reward. Follow these tips for a guilt-free doze:

- Feeling drowsy after lunch? That's perfectly normal and not down to eating too many carbs, as many people believe. In fact, it's the result of a dip in our circadian rhythms, the body's twenty-four-hour cycle of activity, which leaves us craving a snooze at around 3 p.m. So why not make the most of it with a short nap? It could be a great way to prepare for a test or presentation, especially if you study before and after.
- If learning is your goal, opt for a nap of sixty minutes or more, to make sure you include some of that all-important slow-wave sleep that helps us shift memories into long-term storage.
- Even a short nap of five to fifteen minutes can have immediate effects and boost alertness for up to three hours.
- Longer naps can give you a cognitive boost for as long as twenty-four hours, but beware – there's a risk you could wake up after deeper sleep feeling groggy, a phenomenon known as sleep inertia.
- To avoid sleep inertia after a half-hour power nap, drink a cup of coffee just beforehand. You should have plenty of time to nod off before the caffeine kicks in after about twenty minutes or so, and you'll awaken feeling more alert.
- As long as it doesn't stop you sleeping at night, you might want to build napping into your routine. People who nap regularly report a better mood and feel more satisfied after a nap compared to occasional nappers.
- Only got time for a quick nap? Go for it, but opt for a lie-down. Dropping off for a nap takes 50 per cent longer if you're sitting rather than lying.

Some compelling evidence for this comes from one study in which people were either deprived of sleep for thirty-six hours or allowed to sleep normally. They then had to do a learning exercise to test their temporal memory (memory of when events occurred), after which everyone was allowed to sleep normally for two nights. Those who were sleep deprived before learning remembered significantly less, even once their sleep was restored.

Sleeping, then, before you need to learn, is also vital.[38] Finally, having a regular sleep routine also seems to aid memory consolidation,[39] so it's worth keeping good sleep habits.

Effortless learning?

It's clear that sleep helps us to remember what we've been focusing on in our waking hours, but wouldn't things be easier if we could learn while we sleep? In fact, this idea has something going for it: the brain is still listening in to the outside world as we snooze, and there might be ways to tap into this to learn without the effort.

Hints that this may be possible come from experiments that stimulate other senses. In one study participants had to perform a learning task as the smell of roses was wafted around them. If they were then exposed to the same smell during slow-wave sleep, it gave their memory a boost – they were better at remembering what they had learned the next day. The presence of the smell seemed to turbocharge memory consolidation. Other experiments have performed similar tricks with sounds.

This sort of unconscious learning could eventually be used to help us remember complex things like new languages while we sleep – indeed, brain scans show that we continue to process the meaning of words even when we are unconscious.[40]

Influencing the kinds of memories we make in our sleep could have applications way beyond learning, helping us to kick bad habits and even be better people.[41] For instance, smokers in one experiment were exposed while they slept to the smell of rotten fish or eggs at the same time as the smell of cigarettes. The following week, they smoked significantly less (this didn't happen if they were simply exposed to the bad smells when they were awake).[42] Eventually we might even manipulate our memories to change the way we think. Could reinforcing certain memories over others help us to be less selfish, or fairer? Or could triggering specific memories simply help us to wake up happier, always getting up on the right side of bed?

Given the crucial role of sleep in memory formation, an obvious question is whether this could be the elusive function of sleep. But it's not quite so simple. If it were, you would expect that animals with the most complex brains would sleep the most, but this isn't the case. As Steven Lockley and Russell Foster point out in their book *Sleep*, some of the most accomplished sleepers include the brown bat, the giant armadillo and the python, each clocking in at around eighteen hours of sleep per day – and these are by no means the smartest animals in the world. So while sleep is certainly crucial for memory, it's only one part of the story.

CHAPTER 6

The truth about sleep and Alzheimer's

Alzheimer's disease is one of the most pressing mysteries in healthcare. Despite decades of research, we still have a poor understanding of the disease, what causes it, why some people get it and not others, and crucially – how to treat it.

Over the past few years, one piece of the puzzle at least has fallen into place, and that is the intricate relationship between Alzheimer's and sleep. What scientists have discovered is a possible mechanism for the memory problems that come with the disease and, excitingly, a potential path for earlier diagnosis, and even treating some people with this devastating condition.

The signs that sleep might play a role in Alzheimer's have been there for some time. Sleep disturbances tend to precede the disease by several years, so could be a warning sign that something is amiss. And sleep disruption gets worse as the disease progresses.

Given what we know about the importance of sleep and memory, you might find it remarkable that it's taken so long to get to the bottom of this connection in a disease characterized by memory loss. But until relatively recently, we couldn't examine the brains of people with diseases like Alzheimer's as their illness progressed, instead having to wait to look at their brain once they had died.

Now a plethora of brain-scanning techniques mean we can take a detailed look at the brains of people with Alzheimer's while they are still alive, monitor how the signature plaques and tangles in the brain are developing, and see what happens there when people are asked to perform particular tests and challenges.

Sleeping to forget

To investigate the connection between sleep and Alzheimer's disease, in 2015 Professor Matthew Walker and his colleagues conducted a ground-breaking experiment. Scanning the brains of twenty-six older adults who had no history of dementia or sleep problems, the team were able to measure how much beta-amyloid there was – one of the proteins that is often seen building up in the brain of people with Alzheimer's. Specifically, they were looking at an area of the brain called the medial prefrontal cortex (mPFC), which plays an important role in generating slow-wave sleep. As we discovered in the previous chapter, slow-wave sleep is the deep restorative sleep that has been shown to help long-term storage of memories.

Once they had had their brains scanned for the build-up of beta-amyloid, the participants took part in a learning task. They also had their brain waves monitored during a night of sleep, and completed a memory test the following day. The results were astounding. Those people who had more beta-amyloid in the mPFC also had more disruption to their slow-wave sleep. In turn, the more slow-wave sleep disruption they experienced, the bigger the disruption to their memory formation.[43] The more amyloid, the less slow-wave sleep, and the more forgetting – rather than remembering – happened overnight. The team had shown for the first time a mechanism by which poor sleep could be contributing to the memory problems seen in people with Alzheimer's, with amyloid build-up directly disrupting slow-wave sleep. What's more, their research showed that it was the very deepest of slow-wave sleep that was affected, unlike in normal ageing, which reduces slow-wave sleep more broadly –

showing that something peculiar was going on here aside from what we would expect to see in older brains.

Since that astonishing discovery, there has been a proliferation of research on this connection between amyloid, sleep and memory. However, it turned out to be just one part of the puzzle. Yes, Alzheimer's causes sleep and memory problems, and now there was an explanation for why. But poor sleep is also known to precede the onset of the disease. What if a lack of sleep could be triggering the build-up of amyloid itself? After all, research in mice had explicitly showed that if the rodents are deprived of deep sleep, this damaging protein immediately builds up in the brain.[44] Could it be that the same thing is happening in people? If so, getting better sleep could be a promising way to intercept the build-up of amyloid, and potentially delay or even prevent the onset of Alzheimer's in some people.

To find out, Professor Yo-El Ju at Washington State University in Missouri and her colleagues designed a clever experiment. They brought twenty-two healthy people into their sleep lab and monitored their brain waves every ten seconds while they slept with headphones on. Each time they saw that a slumbering participant entered into slow-wave sleep, the researchers would play a sound through the headphones, getting louder and louder until it just managed to rouse the participants out of this deep sleep, but not loud enough to wake them. In this way, the participants slept through the night, but were deprived of the slow-wave sleep implicated in the build-up of harmful proteins.

The next morning, the level of beta-amyloid was measured in their cerebrospinal fluid, the liquid that bathes the brain and the spinal cord. Sure enough, the people who were robbed of slow-wave sleep had significantly higher levels of beta-amyloid than people who had undisturbed sleep, and the more slow-wave sleep disruption, the worse it was.[45] Just one night of poor sleep was enough to lead to amyloid build-up in the brain. The study, and others since then,[46] found too that people who had worse sleep generally also had a build-up of tau proteins, the other key culprit associated with Alzheimer's.

Taken together, these studies suggest that the connection between sleep and Alzheimer's is likely to be a cyclical one. Disrupted sleep leads to a build-up of amyloid, which in turn interferes with sleep, and so on.

Overnight power-cleanse

Around the same time that this research was shedding light on the connection between sleep and Alzheimer's disease, there was another incredible discovery. This breakthrough offered up a long-sought-after purpose for sleep. And it also helps explain that intimate link between sleep and the plaques that build up in the Alzheimer's brain.

This was the discovery in 2013, by Danish neuroscientist Maiken Nedergaard and her colleagues at the University of Rochester, New York, that the brain has its own waste-clearance system. Similar to how the body uses the lymphatic system to move waste from the tissues into the blood, this system uses cells called glia to collect the toxins and metabolic waste produced by your brain cells as they work, and flush it out into the cerebrospinal fluid. The process, which the researchers called the glymphatic system after the cells that do the work, does happen when we are awake, but it becomes turbocharged when we sleep, flushing out ten to twenty times more liquid: as Walker put it in an interview with *New Scientist*, it gives our brain a 'night time power-cleanse'[47] (see the diagram opposite).

A year later, Nedergaard and her team also discovered that during non-REM sleep in particular, the glial cells shrink, creating 60 per cent more space for the fluid to flush through every nook and cranny of the brain.[48] Crucially, one of the toxic by-products being flushed out by the glymphatic system every

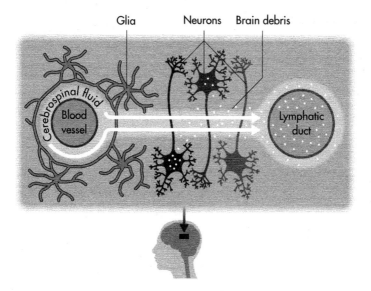

single night when we sleep is the amyloid plaques we see in Alzheimer's disease.

Those studies were conducted on mice, but more recent research has looked at the cerebrospinal fluid of human volunteers as they slept. In 2019, Nina Fultz at Boston University and her colleagues studied the sleeping brains of eleven volunteers and saw for the first time that during non-REM sleep, our brain experiences a pulsing pattern of slow brain waves directly followed by a wave of cerebrospinal fluid. The slow waves of sleep appear to trigger this pulse of fluid, like the spin cycle of a washing machine,[49] showing in more detail just how important slow-wave sleep is for cleaning toxins from the brain.

Early interventions

It is clear that if we want to maximize our chances of preventing Alzheimer's, we need to get serious about sleep, carving out enough time for it in our busy lives. Of course, it is also important to remember that we are talking about a complex disease, and not everyone who has amyloid plaques in the brain goes on to develop Alzheimer's, so the role of sleep is only one part of this giant puzzle.

Even so, now we have this mechanism laid bare before us, it offers the tantalizing prospect that identifying sleep issues could be a way to diagnose Alzheimer's earlier. In 2020, Walker and his colleagues showed that looking at how well people sleep can be a direct predictor of how much beta-amyloid build-up they will have several years later, meaning that sleep could be an early tool to predict when Alzheimer's might strike.[50]

Ultimately, the hope is that treating some of the sleep problems that put people at risk of Alzheimer's will delay and even prevent the onset of the disease. Promisingly, studies with people who have early-stage dementia have shown that treating their sleep disorders can help slow their cognitive decline and delay Alzheimer's by as much as a decade.[51] For some people, cognitive behavioural therapy works well for improving sleep, but for others their sleep problems are very hard to treat with conventional methods, and several research labs, including Walker's, are now investigating more cutting-edge ways to treat sleep disorders and promote this vital, cleansing slow-wave sleep.

One avenue is non-invasive brain stimulation,[52] which uses small electrical currents on the scalp to try to promote slow-wave sleep.[53] Another approach is to deliver auditory tones in synchrony with slow waves during sleep in order to give them a boost.[54] And there is a growing market of gadgets that promise to hack your sleep, and improve the amount of slow-wave sleep you get – although these tend not to have any regulatory approval, so the jury is still out on how well they work. For the rest of us, there's now a better reason than ever to get to bed earlier and let your brain's power-cleanse get to work.

HOW MUCH SLEEP?

How much sleep should you get if you want to try to protect your brain from dementia? One large study from 2020 pooled together over 28,700 people taking part in long-term research projects in England and China and looked at how much people slept, and their cognitive decline during the follow-up period – which amounted to a hundred thousand years between them. They discovered a U-shaped curve, which is to say that people with extreme sleep habits – less than four hours a night or more than ten – had the most cognitive decline in the follow-up period. The effects were especially strong for memory, leading the authors to conclude that cognitive function should be monitored in individuals with insufficient or excessive sleep duration.

We know that too little sleep is bad for memory, but it's not yet clear why too much might be problematic, and it could be possible that people are simply sleeping more as a result of the early stages of dementia or because of other issues that might also predispose them to it.[55] A 2021 study of middle-aged adults suggests that seven hours a night might be the sweet spot – those who got less than six hours were at greater risk of dementia later on than those who got seven.

CHAPTER 7

Being tired destroys your cognitive abilities

Most of us would balk at the idea of getting behind the wheel drunk, but what about when we are feeling tired? Society doesn't condemn it anywhere near as strongly – just take the fact there are no laws to ban it. But perhaps there should be.

We've long known that a lack of sleep leaves us mentally sluggish, but you might be surprised to discover just how much. In 2020, Joanna Lowrie at the University of Dundee, in Scotland, and Helen Brownlow at the Centre for Forensic and Legal Medicine, also in Dundee, set up an experiment to compare the effect of driving when tired to driving after a few too many.

Thirty volunteers did a driving simulation when they were either sober and rested, had been kept awake for twenty-four hours, or had imbibed enough Sauvignon blanc to tip them over the Scottish drink-drive limit of 22 micrograms of alcohol in 100 ml of breath (a similar level to much of the rest of the world). As well as the driving tests, participants had to rate how good they thought their ability to drive was before and after drinking a cup of coffee.

Out of control

Compared to people who were intoxicated on white wine, those who hadn't slept ended up with slower braking reaction times and less control of the car. Some people fared more badly than others – women scored better on the driving test than men on the whole, and those worst affected fell asleep at the wheel in episodes of dangerous 'micro sleeps' that caused them to veer off the road.

Surprisingly, caffeine did little to help. Although coffee is often recommended to alleviate the effects of tiredness when driving, including in the Highway Code in the UK, in this study it had no impact on driving skills, either when people had been sleep deprived or when they had been drinking. Worryingly, in both groups people mistakenly thought that the caffeine hit had improved their ability to drive, giving them a dangerously false sense of confidence.[56]

The findings are particularly important for people doing shift work, who often have to get behind the wheel at night, not only when they are sleep deprived but also when their circadian drive to sleep is at its strongest. In future, the authors of the study suggest, we might consider a change of the law to include driving when sleepy. It could be possible to pull drivers over and test how tired they are by measuring the reaction times of their pupils, as well as to conduct blood tests that can predict sleep loss, although this would be logistically harder to administer. Both techniques are in development. In the meantime, those of us who do drive at night or when we have slept badly should remember that caffeine might make us feel more competent, but that could be an illusion – better to take a nap instead.

Sleepwalking into spring

You don't need to pull an all-nighter to feel the effects of lack of sleep on your cognitive abilities; even a small reduction in sleep can have a big impact. The hour that is lost when the clocks go forward in springtime in the US sees a 17 per cent spike in traffic accidents the following Monday morning (and a 5 per cent rise in heart attacks in the three weeks afterwards, too),[57] suggesting it can take days or even weeks for us to adjust to even an hour less sleep. This is backed up by another study conducted in 2020, which found a 6 per cent increase in traffic accidents in the US in the week after the clocks go forward. One explanation could be the darker mornings – perhaps reduced visibility on the road is to blame? But this seems unlikely given that crashes still increased in the afternoon, and that there was no such surge in fatal accidents when the clocks go back later in the year. As billions of people worldwide are subject to these kinds of clock changes, the public-health impact could be huge, leading the researchers to propose we scrap the practice altogether.[58]

How much sleep is enough for you to confidently get behind the wheel? To find out, Brian Tefft at the AAA Foundation for Traffic Safety in Washington, DC recently conducted the first peer-reviewed study to look at how much a person has slept and their risk of subsequently being responsible for a car crash. He analysed a sample of almost 5,500 traffic accidents, and found that anything less than seven hours a night can put you at serious risk of instigating an accident. Drivers who had had six hours of sleep the night before had 1.3 times the risk of a crash compared to people who had slept for seven to nine hours, while this risk shot up to fifteen times for those who had slept for less than four hours.[59]

It's not surprising that driving becomes so hard when we lack sleep: another recent study found that people who slept less or more than seven to eight hours performed worse overall on a battery of twelve cognitive tests, and sleeping less than four hours the previous night was equivalent to ageing the brain by eight years.[60] Given that people in many populations around the world routinely clock up less than seven hours sleep a night (see Chapter 9), it's clear that shift workers aren't the only ones who should be thinking carefully about whether they are fit to drive.

Questionable judgement

You might be thinking that you'd never get behind the wheel in such a state, so this doesn't apply to you, but the cognitive toll of being tired doesn't stop with our ability to operate heavy machinery. The springtime clock change reveals another problematic effect of sleep on our cognition: a lack of it messes with our morals. Moral awareness is important because it involves the ability to detect morality in others, not merely our own judgements. Using a series of tests, researchers in the US and Singapore recently looked at how morally aware people are when they are sleep deprived compared to when they are rested, and found that a sleep deficit of just two hours led to a 10 per cent drop in people's ability to detect moral elements of

---

HOW TO COPE WITH CLOCK CHANGES

Even an hour less sleep can have a surprising effect on our cognitive abilities, but there are things we can do to minimize the impact of the clocks going forward.

- Adjust slowly. In the days before the clocks change, start going to bed and waking up ten to twenty minutes earlier each day, so you aren't losing the whole hour in one go.
- Make sure you've been getting enough shut-eye in the weeks leading up to the clock change, to avoid starting with a sleep debt that will only worsen the effects of another short night.
- Don't have a lie-in to make up for the lost sleep. Instead, for the next few days get up and out into daylight, which will help to set your body clock a bit earlier.
- Don't skip meals, and don't eat any later than usual, to help your body adjust to the new time.
- If you're struggling to fall asleep earlier, try a hot bath before bed. The drop in body temperature afterwards should help you feel more drowsy.

a scenario they were presented with. And on the Monday after the clocks go forward, there is a steep drop in people searching online for words related to morality, such as 'unethical', 'fraud' and 'honesty', a time when people typically will have skipped about forty minutes of sleep the night before.[61]

This fits with other research that shows how sleep can interfere with our ability to make sound judgements. Military officers and cadets who are suffering from long-term sleep loss find it harder to anticipate moral issues, are more rushed in their moral decisions, and find it harder to conduct sound moral reasoning. Outside of the military, too, people who haven't had enough shut-eye find it harder to make decisions on emotionally charged moral issues, and are more likely to accept solutions that would normally go against their personal moral beliefs. It seems that a lack of sleep leaves us morally depleted, so we should avoid making judgements when we've been burning the midnight oil.

Things get even worse when it comes to our biases. Chronic sleep deprivation has been shown in lab experiments to increase implicit biases towards minority groups, and change how trustworthy we think people are based simply on their facial features.[62] These findings are especially pertinent for those in 'high stakes' professions like police and security officers, where sleep is regularly curtailed but where a routine part of the job involves making snap judgements about how trustworthy people are. Even so, none of us are exempt from the social-cognitive impact of missing out on even a small amount of sleep, so we should handle moral and social decisions with care when feeling tired, and remember just how much sleep affects our judgement – including our own judgement of how tired we really are.

CHAPTER 8

Sleep is a kind of overnight therapy

We've all been there. One bad night's sleep is all it takes to leave us irritable, emotional and flying off the handle about the smallest of things. But while decades of research have been dedicated to looking at what happens to our memories when we sleep, it's only in the past ten years that scientists have really started to think about the role of sleep on our emotions. Now, those working on the subject have created a whole battery of brutal experiments that usually involve depriving volunteers of entire nights of sleep, then subjecting them to all sorts of tests in the name of science. We should thank them for their sacrifice – what we are discovering is not only a fascinating insight into the workings of the sleeping brain, but also a better understanding of our dreams and what they may be for, and crucially, potential new ways to tackle mental-health conditions – from depression to anxiety and schizophrenia.

The connection between sleep and our emotions starts with memory. As we discovered in Chapter 5, sleep plays a vital role in memory formation. For optimal remembering we should learn things within a 'sleep sandwich' – good sleep before and good sleep after. Even so, we only remember a fraction of what happens to us, and nobody knows exactly how the brain decides which memories to hold onto and which to relegate to our forgotten past. What is becoming clear is that sleep plays a role in filtering our memories, and crucially, our sleeping brains prioritize memories that have an emotional component.

Intuitively, the idea that we remember things that are emotionally loaded and have personal significance makes sense – in a day on which you almost got hit by a car crossing the road after a lunch date, it's more useful for your future survival to remember the brush with death than what kind of sandwich you ate. So, when we are well rested, sleep seems to file away memories of things that have a strong emotional component and pays less attention to the mundane.

In the absence of good sleep, however, things get more complicated. After poor sleep, we generally remember less of what we've been learning (which is why cramming for exams is a bad idea). But the tired brain is particularly interested in the types of emotions that accompany our memories. When we sleep badly, we are much more likely to remember things that have a negative emotion attached to them, rather than those that made us feel good. It's as if negative memories are more resistant to the effects of a bad night's sleep.

To demonstrate this in the lab, a group of participants was kept awake for thirty-six hours before having to learn a set of words that were either positive, negative or neutral. They were then allowed to sleep normally for two nights before being tested again. Another group was allowed to sleep normally throughout the whole experiment. People who had got plenty of sleep before learning the words remembered more positive and negative words compared to neutral words two days later – as expected, their sleeping brains prioritized memories that had an emotional component. By comparison, those who were sleep deprived remembered almost 60 per cent fewer positive words, but their memory for negative words was the same as with those who had rested. When it came to negative emotional content, the brain stubbornly held on to it regardless of sleep.

Darker moods

From an evolutionary perspective it would make sense to prioritize remembering negative experiences over the positive, especially at times of stress – times when we would probably have got less sleep. Remembering negative experiences can help us change our behaviour to stop the situation arising again – which could have saved our ancestors' lives by helping them to remember which foods are poisonous, say, or recall the location of a lion attack.

But in modern technological societies, this system might be pushed out of kilter. Artificial lighting, screen-use and a performance culture that puts sleep at the bottom of the to-do list is causing many of us to cut down on sleep, and some experts believe that this scrimping on shut-eye could be keeping us in such a 'survival mode', causing an emotional imbalance that is skewing us towards remembering the negative and leaving us more likely to forget positive experiences. This could be especially true for people with depression, who tend to see their life events as overly negative, and who also often have disrupted sleep.

Even a small amount of missed sleep can darken your mood. In case we needed evidence to prove it, research looking at how lack of sleep affects our temperament found that when people were allowed to sleep for five hours per night for a week, they became significantly more cranky as the week went on. And the effect on our emotions leaves us struggling to cope with the pressures of the day, too. When medical residents were sleep deprived, they found workplace problems excessively difficult to handle, and felt less pleasure in response to things that should have been rewarding.

In this respect, science is catching up with what we know – a lack of sleep messes with our emotions and our ability to cope with stressful situations and decision making. Now we are also getting a picture of what's happening in the brain. When people were put in a brain scanner and made to look at pictures ranging

Prefrontal cortex

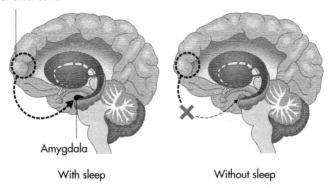

Amygdala

With sleep   Without sleep

from neutral to negative and aversive, those who had scrimped on sleep the night before had a whopping 60 per cent more activation in the amygdala, an area of the brain that processes emotional information – especially in response to the unpleasant images.

Not only that, but the scans revealed much weaker connections between the amygdala and another area of the brain called the medial prefrontal cortex (see the diagram above). Its role is to inhibit activity in the amygdala – helping to dampen down our emotional response and make sure it is appropriate to the situation. So sleep triggers vital activity in areas of the brain that handle our emotional response to negative experiences, possibly resetting our brain so it's ready to deal with whatever the next day throws at us. This in turn enables us to make rational decisions and have a measured emotional response. Conversely, when we miss sleep and short-circuit this process, we are much less able to cope with negative experiences and emotions. Importantly, the pattern of brain activity that we see after poor sleep is similar to that seen in psychiatric disorders that also tend to go hand in hand with sleep problems.

The upsides of dream sleep

The more we discover about the role of sleep in processing our emotions, the more attention is being given to one type of sleep in particular – REM sleep. When we think about the benefits of a good night's sleep, we tend to concentrate on the deliciously restorative, deep sleep that leaves us feeling refreshed in the morning, and that helps to clean the brain and lay down new memories. By comparison, REM sleep seems almost frivolous; it's the time when we have our most fanciful, surreal dreams.

The purpose of dreaming is still hotly debated, but there is growing evidence pointing to REM sleep as the time when this crunching of our emotional baggage seems to be happening. To take one example, people were shown both emotionally rousing and neutral pictures and then either had a ninety-minute nap or stayed awake. Those in the nap group remembered significantly more emotional information afterwards than those who didn't get a snooze. What's more, how much this emotional memory was enhanced was directly related to how much REM sleep they got during the nap, and how quickly they went into REM sleep.

This focus on REM sleep has led some researchers to wonder whether it could be dreams themselves that are actively regulating our emotions. While we do dream in NREM sleep, these dreams tend to be pretty dull. Perhaps the reason our REM dreams are so vivid and emotional is that they are a way of helping us to make sense of our feelings, playing out different scenarios and leaving us better able to make fraught decisions. There is tantalizing evidence this could be the case. One study looked at women who were depressed after going through a divorce, and found that they had more dreams – and more emotionally charged dreams – about their ex-spouse than women going through divorce who were not depressed. However, those who had more of these intensely emotional dreams were also more likely to be in remission from their depression a year later. Their dreams somehow seemed to help them recover from the trauma.

More evidence came in 2021 when Francesca Conte and her colleagues at the University of Campania L. Vanvitelli, in Italy, conducted the first study to compare both waking and dream emotions in good and bad sleepers. They found that people who are good sleepers have a bigger difference in their emotions between when they are awake and in their dreams, with more positive emotions in the day and much stronger negative emotions in the night. Poor sleepers, on the other hand, have a similar level of emotions when awake and when dreaming. One interpretation is that poor sleepers are struggling to process their negative emotions – when we miss out on sleep, the mechanism that helps to process negative emotions from the day isn't working.[63]

Not all studies have linked REM sleep to emotion processing, so we still don't know for sure that this is the case, but the evidence is compelling enough for Matthew Walker and Dr Els van der Helm at the University of California, Berkeley, to suggest that sleep could be a kind of 'overnight therapy'.[64] They believe that as well as sleep helping us to remember things, we

---

CREATIVITY BOOST

When we sleep, the brain makes connections between stored information and new memories that help us make new associations – and result in better creative thinking. This could be why so many people get that aha-moment after sleeping on a problem. Experiments in the lab back this up. After sleep, people find it much easier to find hidden solutions to problems they'd been working on the previous day. This seems to be particularly true of REM sleep. One study found that people were 30 per cent better at solving anagrams after a period of REM sleep compared to NREM.

also 'sleep to forget' the emotional aspect of those memories. Over time, our emotional response to experiences weakens – the amygdala doesn't respond as strongly when we revisit the same memory cues many months later (something we all know from experience – time is a healer). And this seems to happen in large part during REM sleep, as if the emotional 'blanket' surrounding the memory is stripped away at the same time as the actual memory is strengthened.

Sleep and depression

If such findings are right, they could have important consequences for our mental wellbeing, because a failure of this system to work properly could lead to a state of anxiety.

Many mental-health problems and psychiatric disorders involve sleep disruption as a symptom; 90 per cent of people who have depression experience sleep disturbance. Insomnia is a strong risk factor for depression too, and people who are depressed tend to take longer to get to sleep at night, and wake up more often. Intriguingly, they also usually have more REM sleep than most, and enter into REM sleep faster when they do fall asleep.

Similarly, post-traumatic stress disorder (PTSD) often involves nightmares and other sleep problems, and people with REM sleep disruption after trauma are at increased risk of developing PTSD. All this is causing a rethink in our understanding of these mental-health issues. For a long time, people have assumed that those with mental-health conditions who have trouble sleeping were not sleeping because these conditions were keeping them awake. But the emerging science of sleep and emotion has left some scientists thinking that a lack of sleep itself could be causing problems like depression or PTSD, or at the very least putting people at risk of developing them and then worsening the symptoms. They argue that chronic lack of sleep results in an imbalance in the kinds of memories that get encoded in

HOW TO GET MORE REM

REM sleep could play a crucial role in regulating our emotions. There are some things you can do to get more of it.

- Most importantly, try and sleep until you wake naturally rather than using an alarm clock.
- Avoid too much alcohol. It might help us pass out for the night, but it disturbs our sleep and causes us to wake frequently. This could be down to a number of things: alcohol relaxes the throat muscles, interfering with breathing in the night; the diuretic effect means we are more likely to wake up due to the need to pee, or the relaxing effects of the alcohol may simply be wearing off. After a couple of drinks, the amount of REM sleep specifically is also significantly reduced.
- Research shows that watching a disturbing film before bed can mess with REM sleep, so you might want to avoid scary movies before a big day.
- Avoid taking marijuana. This is a known REM sleep suppressant, and anecdotally people report a 'rebound' dream effect, with much more vivid dreams when they stop using it.

the brains of people with depression, causing them to build a picture of their life as filled with negative and neutral events, while erasing the positive experiences.

Given the importance of REM sleep, and the fact that so many of us aren't getting enough sleep, some are going so far as to argue that as a society we might be setting ourselves up for an epidemic of REM sleep loss.

That said, there are other reasons why a lack of sleep could cause symptoms of mental-health disorders. Many of the chemical pathways involved in sleep are also implicated in mental-health and psychiatric problems, and recent genetic studies show an overlap in genes involved in mental-health conditions and in sleep disorders,[65] so there seems to be a genetic component at play too. Add to that the inability to cope with the demands of life when we are super-tired, and it's not surprising that when we are exhausted we also have lower self-esteem, and feel more worried, anxious, frustrated and depressed.[66]

Still, this new understanding of the role of sleep could lead to novel ways to help prevent and even treat some mental-health problems.[67] One another trial across twenty-six universities in the UK, for instance, found that treating students' insomnia was associated with a reduction in paranoia and hallucinations.[68] Well-timed bouts of sleep could also help to process the excessive fear response of people with PTSD.[69]

It is also a wake-up call for anyone who fails to get enough sleep. When you have a big, emotionally fraught decision to make, sleeping on it really could help you see clearly. And making sure you get enough sleep – especially REM – should help you cope with difficult situations and feel more pleasure from the good ones. There are plenty of things you can do to turbocharge your REM sleep (see the box opposite), but the best one is to try to wake up without an alarm clock. We get the most REM sleep at the end of the night, so going to bed early enough that you can wake up naturally is the best way to maximize your REM sleep and get up on the right side of bed.

CHAPTER 9

How much sleep do you really need?

At its very worst, a lack of sleep can kill you. People with an extremely rare disease called Fatal Familial Insomnia (FFI) experience a mild insomnia at first, which worsens rapidly over the next few months until their body and brain deteriorate to the point where they end up in a coma and soon die. It would be unethical to find out how long a healthy human can survive on no sleep, but we know that animals routinely die if they are forced to stay awake for too long. In one classic experiment that deprived rats of sleep, all of them were dead within thirty-two days.[70] Even small amounts of missed sleep can leave you feeling like a zombie. How much, then, do you actually need for optimal functioning?

The ages of sleep

According to standard advice, adults should get between seven and nine hours of sleep a night, although there is huge variability in how much any one person needs.[71] Nobody really knows where these numbers come from, and a look at our recent history hints that sleeping in one chunk of time at night might be a relatively recent idea. Our ancestors may have slept in several bouts, with periods of activity in between. However, the advice that we need seven or more hours seems to fit with studies showing that anything less than this can impair our cognitive functions and lead to other health issues.

HOW CAN YOU TELL IF YOU ARE SLEEP DEPRIVED?

Not everyone needs the same amount of sleep, so going by general recommendations can only help so much. There are various tests used to assess people's sleepiness. One is the Epworth sleepiness scale, which you can fill out online – the score will give you an idea of whether you are getting enough sleep, and can be useful to diagnose disorders such as sleep apnoea, in which people might not realize how many times each night they are waking up. Another way is to look at the kinds of things people experience when overtired. If some or all of the following signs apply to you, it points to a lack of sleep:

- you are dependent on an alarm clock, or another person, to get you out of bed
- you get up late on free days
- you take a long time to wake up and feel alert
- you feel sleepy and irritable during the day
- you feel you need a mid-afternoon nap to function adequately
- you are unable to concentrate and exhibit overly impulsive behaviours
- you crave caffeinated and sugar-rich drinks
- you experience increased worry, mood swings, anxiety and depression

Not only does the amount we need to sleep vary between people, but it will also change for any one person during their lifetime. Newborn babies sleep for as much as nineteen hours a day, but by the time we reach old age we make do with about seven or eight. It doesn't necessarily mean that older people need less sleep, but with age our circadian clock shifts, meaning we wake up earlier in the morning, and would therefore need to be asleep earlier to make up for it.[72] This might be why adults in their sixties report going to bed on average one or two hours earlier than those in their twenties. The circadian window for sleep is also smaller, which means that we might find it harder to sleep for long periods in older age – if older adults are allowed to sleep as long as they like, they tend to sleep for an hour less than younger adults.[73] This doesn't mean that their daytime functioning isn't impaired though. In other words, older people might need just as much sleep, but they find it harder to get.

As we age, our sleep also becomes more fragmented, and these disruptions eat away at the total sleep we get each night, shortening it by about thirty minutes each decade between middle age and old age,[74] which might also explain older adults reporting feeling sleepier during the day.

How much sleep an individual needs seems to be determined by our genes – one gene involved was found to add 3.1 minutes of sleep for every copy of the gene a person has.[75] All this variability has led the US National Sleep Foundation to tweak its sleep recommendations to allow some leeway for individuality. For example, adults should get seven to nine hours a day, but it might be appropriate for some people to get as little as six, and others to sleep for ten.

Quality, not just quantity of sleep is also important. In 2020, Wei Xu and colleagues at Qingdao University in China conducted a review of fifty-one studies[76] looking at the effect of sleep on cognitive decline in people who did not have dementia. They found that ten types of sleep problem – including insomnia, fragmented sleep and sleep apnoea – all increased the risk of developing cognitive disorders, which means that finding ways to treat these sleep problems is more important than ever.

Social jet lag

What about staying in bed too long? You might have heard that too much sleep can lead to a number of diseases, including type 2 diabetes, obesity and heart disease, and drive us to an early grave, but a 2014 study of almost twenty-five thousand people looking into the question found that while the risk of psychiatric illness increased with longer sleep duration, there were no other health effects.[77] It could be a case of cause and effect – people who sleep longer might also be more inactive or have other problems, such as chronic pain, that mean they spend longer in bed.

There's a simple way to find out if you're getting enough sleep for you: don't set an alarm, and just wake up naturally (a luxury many of us can't afford!). How quickly you go to sleep will also offer a clue – if you are out like a light when your head hits the pillow, you are probably running on empty, as it should take around fifteen minutes to doze off.

TIPS FOR BETTER SLEEP

During the day:

- Get as much early morning light as possible, which should bring forward your circadian rhythm, helping you go to sleep earlier. If natural light isn't an option, a light box can help.
- If you must nap, limit it to twenty minutes, to avoid sleep inertia, and don't nap fewer than six hours before bedtime.
- Avoid vigorous exercise too close to bedtime, as this will raise your body temperature. Falling asleep is associated with a small drop in core body temperature, which you don't want to override with exercise.
- Eating within three hours of bedtime can disrupt your sleep, so try to eat earlier where possible.
- Although people respond differently to the effects of caffeine, in healthy adults it has a half-life of five to six hours, so limit caffeine intake in the afternoon.
- Short-term stress disrupts sleep, so resolve conflicts during the day.

If that sounds like you and you need to catch up on sleep, be wary of the weekend lie-in. Social jet lag – where our social and work commitments mean we are up when we should be sleeping, and sleeping when we should be up and at it – can be bad for our health and also leaves us feeling sleepy and sluggish.[78] Going to bed at the same time each night is good sleep hygiene, helping us to get better sleep overall. So if you are feeling the effects of too little sleep, a well-timed nap might be a better option than a lie-in.

One thing we can say with certainty is that it does matter when you sleep. Sleep is controlled by two main drivers. One is our circadian clock – an internal twenty-four-hour timer in the brain that helps drive our daily rhythms of activity. The other is known as sleep pressure, which you can think of as a meter that keeps track of how long it is since you last slept. Sleep pressure builds during the day, making us feel sleepier in the evening, and then diminishes when we sleep. The circadian clock compels us to sleep at night and makes us feel alert during the day. These two drivers of sleep complement each other, which means that at the end of the day, our sleep pressure is strong, and our circadian alertness is low, encouraging us to sleep. If someone is awake when both of these pressures are strong – in other words, they have been awake for a long time and it's also the night time – the effect is bigger than the sum of its parts, making us particularly prone to accidents. As a result, the window between 3 and 6 a.m. is the most dangerous time to be awake.[79]

Further problems arise when people try to live their life out of sync with these strong biological urges to sleep. The most profound effects have been seen in shift workers, who generally get less sleep overall, usually less than five or six hours, even though they try to make up their sleep during the day. That's not surprising when you consider they are working while their body is geared up for sleep and they are trying to sleep while their body

HOW TO KEEP A SLEEP DIARY

Sleep problems often go unnoticed, and we tend to overestimate how much sleep we are really getting. Here's where a sleep diary can help. If you're feeling tired and you can't work out why, this technique gives you an objective sense of your sleep quantity and quality, and can also help you work out what lifestyle factors are disrupting your sleep. All you need is a pen and paper, which you should keep close to your bed – but there are also many templates available to download online. Although they vary, all sleep diaries usually include information such as what time you went to bed; when you went to sleep (this can be the hardest thing to record accurately, and it's better not to clock-watch); whether you woke up in the night, and if so how many times and how long for; what time you woke up in the morning; how you felt the next day; any naps; and details of caffeine, alcohol or medication and exercise you take. After a couple of weeks, you might gain fresh insights into things that are getting in the way of quality sleep.

is totally wired to be awake. Even after an entire career of shift work, people never seem to adjust – their body stays synced to the daytime.[80] And the fact that most shift workers have a rota in which they have periods of night work, and then several days off, only exacerbates the problem.

As well as having a negative effect on general health (the World Health Organization now classifies shift work as 'probably carcinogenic'), living in this way takes a mental toll. A study of over three thousand people in France found that those who had spent at least ten years as shift workers had worse cognitive and memory performance than people who had never done this kind of work. The same has been shown among airline crew.[81] And people who work out of sync with their body's sleep cycles are also at risk of depression. It's perhaps not surprising that divorce rates are particularly high in this group.[82]

To a lesser extent, people who are naturally extreme 'night owls' or 'morning larks' might also feel the effects of having to be up and about at a time that doesn't suit their biology. Perhaps employers could take this into account, giving morning people the early shift and saving the night one for the owls. For those of us who have the flexibility, basing our day around the times we are most alert would also make sense.

Despite having a decent picture of how much sleep we actually need, it seems that, on the whole, people around the world are not getting enough. Looking at data collected through a sleep-tracking app, researchers have found a great variability in sleep from different countries, with residents of only four – New Zealand, the Netherlands, France and Australia – clocking up more than eight hours a night.[83] These countries also scored the highest in another study of global sleep using a different app, along with the UK, Belgium and Finland, although according to that study not one country managed more than eight hours. By contrast, Japanese people consistently seem to be getting little sleep, barely managing six hours.

The fact that so many of us around the globe fail to meet the recommended amount of sleep has caused many researchers to warn that we are living in a global sleep-loss epidemic, which is having serious consequences on our health.

CHAPTER 10

Tiredness can be all in the mind

Feeling ropey after a night of bad sleep? It might be all in your head. As we learned in Chapter 7, burning the midnight oil can play havoc with our cognitive abilities. But thanks to some ingenious experiments we are also discovering that our brain function can be influenced merely by how well we *think* we sleep.

Simply being told you've slept well is enough to trick your brain. In one study, for instance, people with insomnia were given a wearable device to monitor their sleep and randomly told by researchers the next morning that they had had either a good or a bad night's rest. Those who thought they had slept badly ended up less alert and more fatigued than those who believed they had slept well, even if it wasn't true. And those who had been told they had slept well also felt in a better mood, more alert and much less sleepy.[84] Similarly, in another study young people were told they had either above- or below-average sleep quality the night before, which affected how well they scored on measures of attention and executive function.[85]

In general, people are pretty bad at knowing how well they sleep,[86] and around 40 per cent of us believe we have symptoms of insomnia when really we have been asleep. These people have what's known as 'insomnia identity', and simply believing they have slept badly leaves them impaired the next day, and prone to other issues such as depression, suicidal thoughts, anxiety and fatigue.[87]

To monitor our sleep more closely, many of us are turning to fitness trackers which claim to be able to monitor everything from how long we have slept and when, to how much time we spent in each phase, and overall sleep quality. These devices normally rely on how much you move in the night, or on in-built heart-rate monitors. A word of caution, however: many sleep scientists do not believe that these trackers can truly do what they claim – other than being able to tell you a rough number for how long you slept. This might give you a useful baseline to measure sleep over time, but given how suggestible we are to our expectation of sleep, placing too much importance on these scores – especially a bad one – might leave you feeling worse than you need to.

That groggy feeling

Even if you've slept perfectly well, there's another reason you could wake up feeling exhausted: sleep inertia – that groggy morning feeling that has us reaching for the cafetière. The haze of sleep inertia tends to dissipate after half an hour or so, although it can sometimes take several hours to reach full alertness, during which time our brains are less than sharp, and reaction times and decision making are both diminished. In fact, it is a bad idea to get behind the wheel of a car or make any big decisions before you've given your brain time to shake off the remnants of sleep, as during this period our brains are in a similar state to being drunk or as if we've missed a whole night's sleep.

Sleep inertia is particularly pronounced when we wake up during the night, because the circadian drive for sleep is at its strongest, but it will also strike after a longish nap. One way to reduce it could be to set an alarm with a tuneful ringtone. In 2020, researchers in Australia found that a melodic alarm improved people's vigilance on waking, but the same wasn't true for a rhythmic tune.[88] And if you want to wake up alert after a short nap, drink a cup of coffee beforehand, so that the caffeine kicks in just in time when sleep inertia hits.[89]

There is one more reason you might feel dozy regardless of how much you slept. Pay close attention and you might notice that you have periods of focus, followed by an energy lull, consistently throughout the day. Welcome to your ultradian rhythm, which tends to peak every ninety minutes or so, with the lull lasting for about twenty, although this will vary from person to person. Working out which times of day you're most alert and resting in between could be a good way to boost productivity.

TUNE THE MIND FOR BETTER SLEEP

Psychology and sleep are deeply connected. Thinking we have slept well makes us feel better, but feeling good can also promote sleep. Here's how to prepare the mind for a good night's rest:

- Dim the lights around thirty minutes before bedtime. The jury is still out on screens before bed. But playing games or scrolling is a bad idea nonetheless, and might set the mind racing.
- Avoid discussing stressful topics before bed, which will raise the level of stress hormones that can keep you alert.
- Try not to have a smartphone near the bed. Use a traditional alarm, but turn the face away so you don't stress and agonize about the time it takes to get to sleep.
- Go to bed at roughly the same time every night – even at the weekends.
- Get up and do a quiet activity if you can't sleep, rather than worrying about not sleeping.

PART 3

PHYSICAL EXERCISE

If you had to choose just one thing to keep your brain working to the best of its abilities, I would suggest you choose exercise. As a species we evolved to be active, and there is no shortage of evidence that our increasingly sedentary lifestyles, which are so different from those of our ancestors, are taking a toll on our overall health. Conditions including obesity, diabetes and cardiovascular disease are all linked to our propensity to sit, rather than move.

But as we discover in this part of the book, the benefits of exercise – and the dangers of avoiding it – don't stop with the body. Physical activity also has a profound impact on the brain, whether you are doing a single bout of exercise or are a regular fitness fanatic.

One of the most well-studied areas is mood. Anyone who exercises regularly will know the feeling you get after a great workout, and how hard it can be mentally when exercise isn't available, for instance after an injury. And this is backed up by science. As we will see in Chapter 13 exercise improves mood in a variety of ways, and can help alleviate symptoms of conditions such as depression and anxiety.

Working out is also a smart move if you want to get smarter. Keeping active helps children and adults alike with learning, memory, focus and creativity, as we explore in Chapter 12.

Perhaps the most exciting promise of exercise is discussed in Chapter 11: the potential of keeping active to stave off dementia as we age and even to reverse some of its ill-effects, improving cognition in those who already have the disease. We'll also look at the connection between the body and the mind through yoga and meditation in Chapters 14 and 15, and the benefits – as well as the potential pitfalls – they hold.

It's not surprising then, that exercise has been shown in study after study to improve our overall quality of life. All this goes to show that training your body really does provide a thorough workout for the mind. And yet, globally, almost a quarter of adults don't get enough physical activity, nor do 80 per cent of adolescents, and according to the World Health Organization, there has been no improvement in global levels of physical activity since 2001. The problem is especially pronounced in high-income nations, including the US and some European countries. In Germany, just 12 per cent of teens and 46 per cent of adults meet physical activity guidelines.[90] In the US, around half of adults don't do enough cardiovascular exercise,[91] and 78 per cent don't meet the guidelines for both cardio and strength training – instead, both adolescents and adults spend almost eight hours a day being sedentary.[92] Given how young the cognitive effects of exercise take hold, and how important early educational attainment is for later success in life, it seems a no-brainer that we should all get moving more, and get our families moving too. The good news for those who aren't keen on formal types of 'exercise' is that we didn't evolve to run on a treadmill; we just need to find ways to stop sitting still. The brain boost will follow.

CHAPTER 11

Exercise is one of the key ways to prevent dementia

Next time you struggle with the motivation to exercise, try having a chat with the future you. For most of us, exercise is a here-and-now kind of thing. When we lace up our trainers and work up a sweat, it's normally about some kind of immediate goal – getting fitter, looking trimmer, feeling an endorphin buzz.

All of those can be great motivators to get moving, even on days when it feels like a slog. But what if you were told that each run that you go on, each dumbbell you lift or press-up you achieve, could help keep your mind sharp in decades to come? You might start to think of it like long-term savings – a little effort now could lead to huge dividends over the decades.

As we will come to learn in the next chapter, exercise can give the brain a boost in all sorts of ways, from fine-tuning our memory, to spurring creativity and increasing the cognitive processing linked to a higher IQ. But one of the most dramatic things that exercise can do for us individually and as a society is to help our brains to stave off dementia as we age.

We hear a lot about dementia, but what exactly is it? Dementia is an umbrella term that covers a number of medical conditions.

These disorders, the most common of which is Alzheimer's disease, are caused by abnormal changes to the brain, and lead to the decline of cognitive abilities such as memory, problem solving and language that are severe enough to interfere with everyday life. Around 50 million people globally have some form of dementia, and that number is expected to rise to 82 million in the next decade. Alzheimer's disease makes up 70 per cent of all dementia cases but there are several other types of dementia, which have different causes. All of these are a result of some kind of damage to the brain, but we still don't fully understand what causes this damage and how it leads to the symptoms – especially with Alzheimer's disease. For instance, a common tell-tale sign of Alzheimer's is the build-up in the brain of proteins, called beta-amyloid and tau. Amyloid in particular can clump into large sticky plaques and it is thought that this build-up damages brain cells, preventing them from communicating properly – especially in areas important for memory such as the hippocampus.

However, some people have been found to have large amounts of amyloid in the brain but no symptoms. Meanwhile, efforts to treat the build-up of these proteins with drugs have largely failed, and there is currently no cure for Alzheimer's. Because of this, scientists are on the hunt for other explanations for the disease – and new treatments (see Part 6 for more).

Lifestyle choices

Dementia is often seen as a normal or inevitable part of ageing, but that's not the case. In 2020, a group of experts convened by the prestigious *Lancet* journal published a report on the risks of dementia and found that 40 per cent of all cases could be prevented by lifestyle factors such as diet and exercise.[93]

Of course, you can look at that the other way, too – that as much as 60 per cent of dementia cases are unavoidable. Sadly, many people will experience dementia regardless of any choices they make in life, either as a result of unlucky genes or other factors that we don't yet know about. So, of course, we need to continue to look for treatments and cures to help those living with all forms of dementia.

DIFFERENT TYPES OF DEMENTIA

Alzheimer's disease: The most common form of dementia, accounting for 60 to 80 per cent of all cases. Damage and death of nerve cells, probably as a result of signature protein plaques and tangles in the brain, leads to progressive loss of memory and cognitive abilities.

Vascular dementia: The second most common type of dementia. Damage to the brain results from impaired blood flow, often because of a stroke. The effect on thinking skills will depend on how much damage there is, and where.

Frontotemporal dementia: An umbrella term for disorders resulting from nerve-cell loss in the brain's temporal or frontal lobes, causing changes to behaviour and personality, and problems processing language. Some types occur early, often affecting people in their forties.

Lewy body dementia: We don't yet know what causes this type of dementia, but it is characterized by an abnormal build-up of a protein in the brain called alpha-synuclein. These deposits, called Lewy bodies, seem to cause chemical changes in the brain that affect mood, movement, behaviour and memory.

Parkinson's disease dementia: While Parkinson's disease is principally categorized as a movement disorder, an estimated 50 to 80 per cent of people with the condition will develop dementia at some point.

Mixed dementia: Brain changes associated with different types of dementia happen simultaneously; for instance, the plaques associated with Alzheimer's disease occur alongside the blood-flow problems seen in vascular dementia.

Still, the fact that we can do something to prevent so many cases is major, and wasn't always taken as fact. Indeed, it wasn't until the turn of this century that researchers even thought about mental health when they considered what healthy ageing looks like. Until then, mental decline was seen simply as par for the course as we get older. And when you look at the sheer numbers of those suffering with some form of dementia, it quickly becomes clear just how significant that 40 per cent really is. Conditions such as Alzheimer's disease begin in the brain way before symptoms start, sometimes decades earlier, so finding any way to prevent the damage is doubly important. What's more, prevention isn't everything. Even finding ways to delay mental decline can have a huge impact – according to some estimates, delaying the onset of dementia by five years would slash overall incidence of the disease by a third.

So what works? As we will discover throughout this book, there are many things that have been proven to flex our mental muscle, but exercise is one of the most promising.

Compelling evidence that exercise keeps the brain youthful comes from one study which showed that the brains of older people who did moderate physical exercise looked ten years younger than the brains of people who didn't exercise. The researchers, from the University of Miami, tested the memories of 876 people with an average age of seventy-one and also analysed their brain health using MRI scans. Those who exercised did better on the tests at the start of the study, but also scored significantly better after five years than those who didn't exercise.[94] The exercisers also had better cognitive processing – their cogs were turning faster than those who didn't work out. Interestingly, however, the team only saw the effects if people began exercising before any initial symptoms of cognitive decline. So, exercise can help, but it is unlikely to reverse the course you are already on. Another reason why the sooner you start the better.

While results like these are encouraging, the relationship between exercise and cognitive function isn't absolutely clear cut. In a similar way as with diet, it can be difficult to tease out the effect of lifestyle factors such as exercise on specific outcomes like brain health or dementia risk because a lot of the things we do are so closely interconnected. It might be the case, for instance, that people who do more exercise also have better genes involved in brain health, or are more likely to take healthy eating seriously as well. While it is possible to remove some of these confounding variables from studies, they can get in the way of obtaining the clear results we are after. One way to get a sense of the impact is to pool together the results of lots of different studies that might be a bit smaller than we'd like or only looked at specific groups of people, and see whether, taken together, their results give us a better idea of what direction the evidence is pointing in.

Two of these so-called meta-analyses have been carried out in recent years, looking at the effect of exercise on cognition. One pooled fifteen studies totalling over thirty thousand participants, who were followed up for anything from one to twelve years. It found that regular exercise lowered the risk of cognitive decline by almost 40 per cent. Even low to moderate exercise was beneficial. The other analysis included forty-five different studies and a hundred thousand people and lasted as long as twenty-eight years. It found that exercise reduced the risk of developing cognitive problems by 20 per cent, when people did regular, moderate or high-intensity exercise.

Those results are good news for anyone who already exercises or those hoping to get fit in a bid for a healthy brain. What's particularly encouraging is the finding that even moderate exercise can be beneficial. You don't have to be running a marathon a week to get the brain benefits.

It is worth keeping in mind, however, that, as is often the case in science, not all studies agree on these benefits. Large, randomly controlled trials are the gold standard for scientific research, and one such study enrolled over one thousand six hundred older people aged between seventy and eighty-nine and got them to either follow a moderate exercise programme for two years

Exercise intensity	Heart rate (beats per minute)	Training benefits for the brain
Maximum	171–190 bpm	Boosts levels of BDNF – a protein which helps grow new brain cells, relieves symptoms of anxiety
Hard	152–170 bpm	Helps grow new brain cells, improves mood
Moderate	133–151 bpm	Keeps the brain young, improves memory, improves cognitive processing and helps prevent depression
Light	114–132 bpm	Increases brain volume, reduces risk of cognitive decline

or enrol in education workshops. Unfortunately, there was no apparent difference in cognitive impairment or dementia between the two groups after the time was up, except in those who were over eighty or did very little physical activity beforehand. So, we still need more research to work out exactly who benefits most from exercise when it comes to dementia. Even so, on balance, the body of research is compelling, and according to the *Lancet* group, we could reduce worldwide prevalence of dementia by 3 per cent through regular physical exercise.

The fitness advantage

So, what is it about exercise that brings the benefits? There are several possible explanations, and the answer is likely to be some combination. Perhaps the most well-understood link between exercise and offsetting dementia is what we know about the effects of exercise on the body, which in turn affect the brain.

The brain is ravenous, as we discovered in Part 1. It burns through a huge amount of energy and requires a constant supply of oxygen and nutrients to be delivered though the circulatory system. Exercise helps keep this network of blood vessels healthy and blood pressure low. This is important because studies have shown that high blood pressure can damage blood vessels, has been linked to a reduction in cognitive performance and is also a risk factor for dementia. So, exercise might be keeping the whole system working well while feeding the brain.

HOW MUCH EXERCISE IS ENOUGH?

Exercise is one of the best things you can do to prevent dementia, according to a leading Alzheimer's charity. They recommend that each week, you should aim for either:

- 150 minutes of moderate aerobic activity, such as brisk walking, riding a bike or pushing a lawnmower; or,
- 75 minutes of vigorous aerobic activity, such as jogging, fast swimming or riding a bike up a hill.

You should also build in some resistance activities that require strength and work your muscles twice a week, such as:

- digging in the garden; or, exercises, such as push-ups and sit-ups. Alternatively, take part in activities that are both aerobic and include resistance, such as football, running, netball or circuit training. And you can start slowly, with as little as ten minutes at a time.

Exercise also reduces the risk of diabetes and obesity, both strong risk factors for dementia later in life. Being obese aged forty is estimated to increase the risk of dementia by over 70 per cent,[95] and scans of the brains of obese people show alterations to the structure and function of the brain. That's especially true in middle age: conversely to the study that showed the brains of older people who exercised looked ten years younger, scans of obese people's brains can look ten years older than they should be.

As with many lifestyle choices we make, genes seem to play

an important role, too. Research published in 2020 looking at the effect of exercise and diet on the brains of twins found that the presence of certain genes influences how much impact our exercise regimes will have on mental muscle as we age. That means that while 'good' genes can help keep your brain young, you need to make the right lifestyle choices, such as diet and exercise, to see the effects. On the flip side, the same lifestyle choices are likely to have much less of an effect in people who don't have the right genetic makeup.[96]

This genetic research, led by neuroscientist Dr Sandrine Thuret also hints at a very different way that exercise could be protecting our brains as we age. Until recently, it was believed that adults could not produce new brain cells – we only lose them as we age – but we now know that's not the case; it's just that this neurogenesis in adulthood only happens in a few select areas, the most important being the hippocampus.

The hippocampus is key to learning, emotions and memory, and according to Thuret, by the time we reach fifty, we will have replaced all the neurons that we were born with in this brain region.[97] She and others have found that these new neurons play a vital role in memory and learning, and that one of the key ways to promote the growth of these new cells is through exercise, as well as what we eat (for more on neurogenesis, and how to grow new brain cells, see Chapter 16).

Exercise also reduces inflammation, as well as decreasing damage by free radicals, both of which could reduce amyloid build-up.

Finally, hormones might be involved, too. People with Alzheimer's disease often have low levels of a hormone called irisin, produced by muscles when we exercise. A study in mice in 2019 found that blocking the hormone caused memory and learning problems, which could then be restored by reintroducing it.[98] So, one day it might even be possible to swallow a pill that artificially boosts these hormones, giving us the beneficial effects of exercise without the effort. For now, a lot more research is needed before we can tease out exactly what is going on, and the best way to get the benefits of exercise is, well, to exercise.

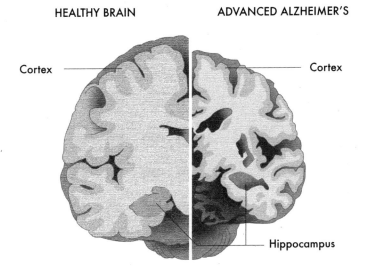

HEALTHY BRAIN   ADVANCED ALZHEIMER'S

Cortex   Cortex

Hippocampus

Exercise that counts

The question, then, becomes which kind of exercise is best, and how much we need to do. Aerobic exercise seems to be the key if we want to get blood pumping to the brain,[99] but as we saw earlier from those meta-analyses, even moderate exercise is enough, including things like a brisk walk or just mowing the lawn.[100]

There are hints that higher intensity is better, however. One study of Swedish women found that those who were fitter in middle age were protected from age-related memory loss later on. Their cardiovascular fitness was measured using stationary exercise bikes and they were followed up more than forty years later. In those who were rated as having high fitness levels, the onset of dementia was delayed by nine and a half years, on

THE TEN BEST THINGS YOU CAN DO TO REDUCE YOUR RISK OF DEMENTIA NOW

1. Not smoke. If you do smoke, try to quit. Even giving up late in life can reduce dementia risk.
2. Find work or hobbies that challenge your brain. People who do cognitively challenging jobs tend to show less cognitive decline before retirement, and countries with an earlier age of retirement have been found to have a bigger drop in cognitive performance.
3. Take regular exercise. This can prevent dementia by lowering the risk of obesity and diabetes, and possibly helping new brain cells to grow.
4. Socialize often. Social contact seems to boost cognitive reserve, a kind of cushion against the effects of ageing on the brain.
5. Reduce alcohol consumption. We've known about the link between alcohol and dementia for decades. You should limit consumption to twenty-one units per week.
6. Keep blood pressure low. Treatment for high blood pressure (hypertension) is the only known effective preventive medication for dementia.
7. Try to avoid head injuries. Every brain injury from things like car accidents and contact sports increases the risk of dementia. This includes even mild injuries such as concussion.
8. Wear a hearing aid when needed. Hearing loss is closely linked to cognitive decline, but only in those people who don't wear a hearing aid.
9. Eat a healthy diet. The World Health Organization recommends that a Mediterranean diet has the potential to help prevent dementia, and certainly won't do any harm.
10. Avoid air pollution where possible. Pollution in the air seems to have a part to play in dementia, possibly because it damages blood vessels to the brain, or causes other cardiovascular problems.

average, compared to those with medium fitness. Whatever your exercise goals, key to keeping it up will be to find something you enjoy that also gets the heart pumping, and then you should start as soon as possible. Not only will your mind feel sharper today; the future you will thank you, too.

CHAPTER 12

Exercise amps up your brain power

With our big brains and highly complex societies, we humans like to think of ourselves as scoring pretty highly, if not right at the top, of the intelligence stakes. And yet our ability for invention and innovation has left us in a bit of a bind. Thanks to our modern-day technologies, most notably the internet, we can now find pretty much everything we need to survive, from our next meal to our next lover, from the comfort of our couches. We might feel pretty pleased with ourselves, but this way of life isn't just thickening our waistlines and driving us to an early grave, it's blunting our intellect too. Not so smart after all.

The wide-ranging consequences of sitting too much and moving too little are not new. Shocked by the weight of the evidence against inactivity, back in 2008 one group of researchers pondered:'Could something as ordinary as sitting in chairs be plausibly grouped among other major health hazards?'[101] If the standing-desk revolution is anything to go by, the answer to that question is now a resounding 'yes'. Sitting has been branded 'the new smoking' in the media, not least because it seems we can't entirely undo the damage done by a day's worth of sitting, simply by going for a daily jog. We evolved to be active for most of the day, and avoiding the lure of the sofa is one of the simplest things we can do for our health.

EPIGENETIC CHANGES

Over the last two decades, we've come to realize that the environment can have a powerful impact on our genes. It doesn't change the genetic code itself, but can switch certain genes on and off, changing the way they work. These so-called epigenetic changes can come about because of our lifestyle choices, and have therefore added another layer to the long-standing nature vs nurture debate. When it comes to the brain, it seems these tweaks to our gene activity can affect brain plasticity, brain function and the growth of new brain cells, and one theory is that exercise could cause this type of change in the way genes work – impacting on brain function.

As for the cognitive benefits of keeping moving, even the ancient Greeks suspected that a healthy body led to a healthy mind. Hippocrates is believed to have said that 'If we could give every individual the right amount of nourishment and exercise, we would have found the safest way to health', although he had no way of knowing quite what he was on to. Thanks to research over the last couple of decades, we now know that keeping active can improve all sorts of thinking skills, from memory and attention, to overall academic achievement in children, and those all-important executive functions – a suite of cognitive skills that are used to control other cognitive processes and behaviours, and include forward planning and self-control. There's no denying that to stay sharp it's important to stay active.

Intriguingly, we are also coming to realize that exercise isn't created equal; different types of movement affect our cognition in different ways. Just as we might choose Pilates to lengthen muscles and yoga to get flexible, running to get fit and weightlifting to get strong, the type of physical activity we choose can sculpt and strengthen the brain just as it does the body.

Aerobic advantage

One key way that exercising is thought to flex your mental muscle is by increasing blood flow to the brain, so it's not surprising that aerobic exercise, the kind that gets the blood pumping, has been shown time and again to be especially effective. It can boost memory and attention, and also leads people to make fewer errors of judgement, as if the brain is better at monitoring itself. One line of thinking, backed up by several studies, is that aerobic exercise leads to the development of new blood vessels in the brain and promotes the growth of new neurons,[102] particularly in the hippocampus, which is crucial to memory. More blood flow to the brain also means there's more opportunity to pump around proteins and other molecules that we know are produced during exercise and that are also involved in the growth of these new brain cells. The muscle contractions that happen with both aerobic exercise and resistance training also cause the release of various molecules into the bloodstream that are known to act on the brain. The most important of these seems to be BDNF, a protein that plays a key role in neurogenesis.

Because the brain develops so fast in childhood, much of the research in this area has focused on children as well as older adults (who also see much more rapid changes to their brain, but in the other direction). These are the times in our lives when the influence of environmental factors, such as exercise, are especially strong. However, for younger and middle-aged adults, the results are more mixed.

Around school age, our brains undergo rapid development, building circuits and connections that allow us to master new skills like controlling our behaviour, multitasking and staying focused in spite of distractions. During this crucial window, the brain is particularly sensitive to the impact of moving our bodies, and many studies show that for school-aged children, keeping active can be transformative. Inactivity and poor fitness are associated with worse academic performance in children as well as lower scoring on standard cognitive tests. However, both single bouts of exercise and regular exercise routines have been shown to improve academic achievement as well as cognitive function and attention.

DID EXERCISE CREATE OUR COMPLEX MINDS?

There's no doubt that having a fit body can lead to a healthy mind, with research showing that exercise can give us all sorts of cognitive boosts and even help to keep dementia at bay. But why? Such is the power of exercise on the mind that some scientists believe we might be thinking about it back to front – exercise doesn't just help our mind perform better, but could be the very reason that the complex human brain evolved in the first place. Humans are better built for endurance than our close relatives, and there seems to be a link between the brain size of mammals and their ability for endurance. It could be that, as our fitness evolved, a by-product was our smarter brains. So, exercise may be the very thing that made us so smart, and that ultimately made you *you*. Such a rethink should help us all to embrace regular exercise, whatever our age.

Exercise changes children's brains too,[103] and those who are fitter often have larger brain areas involved in information processing and relational memory (the type of memory that involves forming associations – for instance, putting a name to the face of someone you met a week ago at the same time as remembering what you talked about and where it all happened).

Children's perception, creativity, maths and verbal tasks all improve with increased physical activity, too, and exercise can help improve cognitive performance in children with attention deficit hyperactivity disorder (ADHD). All this is ample proof of just how important it is to include movement throughout the school day; even a quick burst can help children to focus on tasks. When a lesson is broken up by ten-minute 'energizers', pupils pay more attention afterwards and even make fewer mistakes. But in spite of the obvious benefits of exercise for kids, we know that many children fail to reach the recommended daily guidelines.

Pumping iron

For adults, resistance training – where your muscles are working against a counterweight – seems to be a good choice for staying sharp. As well as promoting BDNF, it can trigger the release of another molecule called insulin growth factor 1 (IGF1), which enhances the growth and survival of neurons, and has been linked to good cognitive performance. Strength training also leads to changes in the brain associated with improved executive function.

It would be a mistake to think that lifting weights should be left to the young: when older women with mild cognitive impairment (MCI) who were therefore at risk of developing Alzheimer's disease did resistance training twice a week for six months, they scored better on tests of attention and memory than those who did aerobic exercise or stretching. Grip strength, which is a good proxy for overall muscle strength, has also been shown to boost memory and reaction times[104] as well as spatial and verbal cognitive skills in people over sixty-five,[105] and it can increase attention and reasoning skills. In fact, the effects of muscle on the mind are so strong that it can even be used as a predictor of cognitive decline – if you lose your grip strength, your thinking power will probably follow suit.[106]

Happily, many of the improvements we see with resistance training can be long lived, lasting a year or more after the training period ended. And you don't need to be pumping iron in the gym – working against your own body weight, for instance doing press-ups and squats, should be enough.

How much exercise is enough to train the brain? One

HACK YOUR EXERCISE FOR THE BEST BRAIN BOOST

1. There is no one specific best way to boost memory-enhancing BDNF production, but the general formula seems to be: intensity + duration + frequency. So go hard, go long and go often for the best results.

2. If you have the option, choose open-skill activities that keep us on our toes, such as badminton, hockey and football, which require us to constantly adapt to a changing environment. Compared to closed-skill activities such as running, which are very predictable and within our control, they lead to a bigger BDNF boost – this is thought to be because they require more attention (and possibly because they are more fun!).

3. If you're revising for a test, try learning on the go. In one study of people memorizing new vocabulary in Polish, participants remembered more new words if they walked while they studied.

4. No need to over think it: a single bout of exercise is enough to boost executive functions, thinking speed, attention and memory, as well as a measure of general knowledge.

5. Struggling with self-control? Exercise can help. One study found that just fifteen minutes of moderate exercise reduced cigarette cravings – and even dampened down brain areas that drive the urge.

---

compelling review looking at studies of older adults found that exercise lasting for forty-five minutes to an hour, over a period of at least six months, was the most beneficial for cognition. To get the most cognitive bang for your buck out of one hard workout, it should last for between eleven and twenty minutes – doing any extra didn't seem to increase the effect. Coincidentally, the biggest cognitive benefits were also seen between eleven and twenty minutes after exercising. In the ten minutes straight after, cognition took a dip, so if you are exercising for the brain-boosting effects, give yourself ten minutes to recover first before getting to work.

While this is the best advice we have for now, in reality we don't yet know the best 'dose' of exercise for the mind, so these findings should be taken with a small pinch of salt. What is clear is that you should try to avoid long periods of sitting on chairs. One way to do that is to find more active ways of sitting. Hunter-gatherer societies, which are a good proxy for the way we evolved to live, spend hours a day resting in squatting positions that engage the muscles of the legs and the core. So why not try reading the rest of this section on your haunches. Failing that, get up for regular breaks. And for optimum effects, choose a range of different activities that will give both your body and your brain a well-rounded workout.

CHAPTER 13

Exercise can boost your mental wellbeing

By now you have probably started to notice a pattern: exercise and brain health go hand in hand. So it will come as little surprise to hear that working out can be hugely beneficial to our moods too. In fact, that's somewhat of an understatement, with studies suggesting that exercise can be as good as, if not better than, standard treatments we have available for certain mood disorders.

There is so much research on the ways that exercise affects our mental wellbeing that, to make sense of it all, it can be helpful to think about different categories of studies. First, there are those that look at the effects of exercise on general mood, compared to those that are specifically trying to understand how it might affect symptoms of anxiety or depression.

Another big distinction is between studies that look at the effects of a single bout of exercise, compared to a longer, more regular exercise regime. In other words, is one run enough or do you need to be a dedicated workout bunny?

Feel-good factor

Let's start with general mood. Can exercise help you feel more positive, regardless of any mental-health conditions? You've probably heard of the runner's high, and the evidence is pretty strong that exercise leaves people feeling more positive for several hours. But the problem with a lot of research on exercise and mood is that it's done in a lab, which of course can be quite artificial – you might feel very different after a jog in the park compared to cycling on a stationary bike with a room full of scientists watching you sweat. So one review of studies looked specifically at how people felt when they exercised in their natural habitat. On the whole, it found that exercise boosted positive feelings and left people feeling more energetic.[107]

When it comes to mood disorders, not all studies agree. There is strong evidence that exercise can be an effective treatment for mild and moderate depression, on its own or in combination with other treatments, especially in adolescents.[108] But in adults, some of the research is more mixed.

There are also questions about how much exercise you need to do to get these effects. Much of the research suggests that more exercise is better, but many studies are too small for us to draw firm conclusions, and certainly too small to be able to tell you which kind of exercise is the best. That's important, because it's one thing to tell people that exercising can help their mental health, and that they are free to choose whatever works for them, and quite another if they need to be prescribed specific exercises for a certain duration to see an effect. In other words, is exercise a universal medicine? Or is it more like a medicine cabinet, and different people need to be prescribed specific types in precise doses?

To get to the bottom of all these questions, in 2018 Sammi Chekroud and his colleagues at the Oxford Centre for Human Brain Activity at Oxford University, in the UK, conducted the biggest study on the subject to date. They analysed information from 1.2 million people, from all across the United States, that had been collected over several years from a phone survey regularly conducted by the US Centers for Disease Control and Prevention (CDC). As well as exercise habits, the survey asked people about lots of other things, such as age, race and sex, as well as their physical and mental health – including whether or not they had ever had depression. This meant the team could compare the effects of exercise on depression, and also take into account other factors that might be responsible. The participants were specifically asked for how many days in the last month they had experienced poor mental health – including things like depression, stress and low mood.

Symptoms slashed

What they found was quite staggering. Compared to people who didn't exercise, those that did had 43 per cent fewer days of poor mental health in the past month, and the effect was larger in people with a previous diagnosis of depression. This beneficial effect of exercise on mental health was seen no matter the age, gender, race or income of the person.

These findings chime with a report published by the Exercise is Medicine public health initiative from the American College of Sports Medicine in Indiana. The report summarizes all the scientific evidence on exercise and health, including its impact on the brain, and found exercise to be an effective prevention tool against depression. For instance, one review of over thirty studies that followed people over long periods of time found that the more exercise people did, the less likely they were to experience depression later on. Even small amounts of exercise were beneficial – 150 minutes per week had an effect.[109] But for people who did thirty minutes of physical activity every day, the reduction in the odds of experiencing depression was slashed almost by half. On the flip side, sedentary behaviour seems to raise the risk.

The evidence is compelling, then, that exercise can reduce the risk of depression, but there is good news for people who already have a diagnosis, too. One 2014 review conducted by Swedish researchers found consistent evidence that exercise can help as a treatment for depression in adults, reducing the symptoms to the same extent as other interventions like cognitive behavioural therapy, or antidepressants.[110] Exercise also seems to have a significant impact on reducing symptoms in young people who have clinical depression.[111] Even so, the challenge remains that it's not always easy for people with depression to get out and exercise.

WHAT IS ANXIETY?

Anxiety disorders are the most common types of mental-health problem, and there are hundreds of studies looking at whether exercise can help. Anxiety is a term we're so familiar with, but what actually is it? The Exercise is Medicine report defines it as 'a noticeable, psychophysiological emotional state, which is most often characterized by feelings of apprehension, fear or expectations of fear, worry, nervousness and physical sensations arising from activation of the autonomic nervous system (e.g., increased muscle tension, elevated heart rate, sweating)'. This is a normal human emotion, part of the 'fight or flight' response that helps us to deal with threats, but it becomes pathological, resulting in clinical anxiety or an anxiety disorder, when our thoughts and actions change in this way even when there isn't an obvious cause, or when our response is disproportionate and unmanageable. With increasing pressures and stress in the way we live, feelings of anxiety are common even in those who don't have a clinical disorder.

For those of us who experience anxiety, exercise intuitively feels like a good way to help clear the head. Whether it's a one-off session, or a regular habit, exercise can help both those people who have been diagnosed with clinical anxiety disorders, and those who are simply feeling fraught. In fact, here too, exercise has been shown to be at least as effective, if not more so, than standard care anxiety treatments.

Power move

Pounding the pavements is one option, but weightlifting is a real heavy-hitter in the feel-good stakes – strength training has been found to reduce anxiety in otherwise healthy adults, help ease symptoms of depression in those with a diagnosis of the condition, and also boost self-esteem.

The potential benefits of exercise on mood, then, are pretty impressive – for a general mood boost, as well as for those with depression and anxiety. In some cases, it's as good as the treatments and drugs we normally use, although you shouldn't stop taking any medication without talking to your doctor. But if exercise really is medicine, then we must return to the important question: what type – and dose – is optimal?

In the large study conducted by Sammi Chekroud and his team, all types of exercise were associated with a reduction in mental-health burden, but some more so than others. The strongest link was for team sports, then cycling, aerobic exercise and gym workouts. Even doing household chores counted – reducing the number of poor mental-health days by almost 10 per cent. And yoga and mindfulness exercises were found to be more beneficial than walking (more on mindfulness later on in chapter 15). The benefits were comparable, and often bigger, than other predictors of good mental health, such as a better education or higher household income.

Peak performance

The researchers also discovered that more isn't always more. An exercise duration of thirty to sixty minutes – peaking at around forty-five minutes – was associated with the lowest mental-health burden, for most exercises. In some types of exercise, working out for much longer than that seemed to undo all the benefits and people at times ended up with worse mental health than those who did no exercise at all. Take jogging, for instance: the peak mental-health benefits came after about forty-five minutes, before getting worse again. For cycling, it peaked at forty-five but then stayed pretty flat thereafter.

Something similar seemed to be going on when the researchers looked at how many times a week people exercised. Those who trained between three and five times a week saw bigger benefits to their mental health than those who exercised less than three or more than five times. This was true for all intensities of exercise, although, as a general rule, vigorous exercise proved more beneficial than moderate or light. Overall, people exercising two to six hours per week had the lowest reports of poor mental health.

This large study wasn't perfect. It was cross-sectional, which means that it looked at a population at a particular point in time, rather than a trial or intervention, which would look at people's mental health before and after embarking on a fitness regime. That means we can't definitely say that the exercise *caused* the effects, rather than representing mere correlation. The study also relied on people's self-reports of exercise and their mental wellbeing, which can be unreliable. More research, for instance, using passive monitoring with a wearable fitness tracker could help deal with some of these issues.

Even so, the study was large and the finding that you don't need to be doing masses of vigorous exercise a week should be a boon to anyone interested in getting started. Just two hours seems to be enough.

Team player
We don't yet know exactly how exercise triggers such a profound effect on mental health – but there are a few prominent ideas. For a start, it makes sense that Chekroud and his colleagues found team sports to be apparently most beneficial since we know from other studies that social activity promotes resilience to stress and

reduces depression (see Part 5 for more on this). The social side of team sports could also help to reduce the social withdrawal and feelings of isolation that often go hand in hand with depression and other mental-health issues.

We've also seen in other chapters that exercise can boost the production of neurotransmitters in the brain, such as GABA and glutamate, chemicals that help brain cells talk to each other efficiently. While this seems to improve memory, it could also play a role in mood, because low levels of both of these neurotransmitters are implicated in depression.[112] And exercise has been shown to directly boost neurotransmitters that are tightly implicated in mood and wellbeing,[113] such as dopamine – the so-called reward chemical in the brain – leading to the feeling of euphoria or 'runner's high' that some people can get with exercise. Just five minutes of dancing, for instance, has been shown to lift people's mood, and the activity also releases endorphins into the bloodstream.[114]

All things in moderation

Inflammation could be another route. One small recent study got sixty-one healthy university students in Canada to exercise at different intensities for six weeks – either high-intensity interval training (HIIT), moderate continuous exercise or no exercise at all – and looked for changes in their reports of depression, anxiety and perceived stress. They also looked for chemicals that are indicative of inflammation in their blood (see Chapter 25 for more on the role of inflammation on mental health, especially depression). The research team not only found that depression rapidly increased in the group that didn't exercise, but so did levels of pro-inflammatory chemicals, whereas the opposite was true in the group that did moderate exercise. Interestingly, the HIIT group had less depression at the end of the study, but had higher perceived stress levels as well as some pro-inflammatory chemicals, leading the researchers to conclude that moderate exercise is the best, and that exercise could help to assuage symptoms of depression by reducing inflammation.[115]

BATH-TIME BRAIN BENEFITS

For some people, exercise isn't an option. Knowing that antidepressants don't work in a third of those who try them, Johannes Nauman and his colleagues at the University of Freiburg in Germany have been working on other treatments that have fewer potential side effects. They wondered whether hot baths could work by restoring the circadian rhythms that are often off kilter in people with depression. In 2017, they conducted a small study showing that taking a long hot bath in a spa, followed by half an hour wrapped in towels and hot water bottles, reduced symptoms of depression on a commonly used scale by three points compared to a control group who were exposed to a green light instead. To take the idea further, they decided to compare the hot baths to something with known benefits for depression: exercise. Forty-five people with moderate to severe depression either took a long afternoon bath twice a week and then rested with hot water bottles for twenty minutes, or did an exercise routine for forty-five minutes or so. After eight weeks, those taking the hot baths had a six-point reduction in their depression scores on average, compared to three points for those who were exercising. The results have yet to be peer reviewed, but the implications of this research are good news for anyone who likes a long hot soak in the tub.

Rather than worry too much about the specific mechanisms at play, you might be better off just thinking about the beneficial effects on the brain as a whole.

One final thing to consider when you think about the effect of exercise on mental health is how you feel not just afterwards, but also while you are exercising. Unsurprisingly, perhaps, studies show that people who are made to do tough levels of exercise in lab experiments experience a dip in their mood – put simply, they don't enjoy it. And how you feel when you exercise is going to have a big effect on whether you stick with it in the long term. So while the promise of a mental pick-me-up after a workout might help motivate you, the real key is to find something that you truly enjoy, whether that's a dance class, a team sport or a jog in the woods – do that, and you're more likely to be smiling afterwards, too.

CHAPTER 14

Yoga can change your brain and calm the mind

Early on in the coronavirus pandemic, when the UK first went into lockdown, I found myself faced with what one *New York Times* reporter called the problem of 'two parents, two kids, two jobs, no childcare (and no end in sight)'.[116] It was an extremely stressful time, and my husband and I would take shifts to work while the other looked after the children, catching up by working long into the night. Fortunately, during that time, I also made one other change to my lifestyle, one that I believe was key to getting through that grind: I decided to do a little yoga, every day.

I found a free thirty-day yoga programme online, and vowed to do around twenty minutes every evening as soon as the children were in bed. I made myself do it – often reluctantly – regardless of the mountain of work and chores waiting for me on the other side. And without fail I stepped off the mat a short time later feeling calmer, less stressed, clear headed, more focused and energized. You could easily put the effect down to the fact I'd given myself a break from all that was going on, or even simply because I was doing a form of exercise, which we know can be so beneficial for the mind. But there seems to be something special about yoga itself that was doing my mind some good.

The amount of research into the effects of yoga on the brain has shot up in the last five years, which is possibly a reflection of its growing popularity in the West. One survey from 2016 estimates there were 36.7 million people practising yoga in the US, up from 20.4 in 2012.[117]

Most people in the survey seemed to be chasing a yoga body rather than inner peace, citing fitness, health and flexibility as their motivation for taking up the practice, closely followed by stress relief.

More than just stress relief

They'd be right about the stress part – there is now plenty of evidence that yoga improves mood and reduces stress,[118] but the mental wellbeing afforded by regularly rolling out the mat doesn't stop there. Even a single session of yoga has been shown to increase levels of positive emotions such as tranquillity and revitalization, while decreasing feelings of exhaustion.[119] It can also enhance cognitive performance, including reaction times and working memory.[120] And yoga has been found to reduce symptoms of depression and anxiety in a range of populations.[121]

So what is it about yoga that makes it so beneficial for the mind? First, a word of caution: there are many different kinds of yoga. Some types can feel like a pretty intense workout, whereas with other styles you'd struggle to raise your heart rate. But what stands all yoga apart from other forms of exercise is that it aims to unite the mind and the body. The physical postures are intended not as the end goal, but as a way of occupying one's thoughts and liberating the mind.

Regardless of the type you choose, all forms of yoga involve attention to breathing, too, as well as some element of meditation, or what neuroscientists sometimes call an 'active attentional component'. Perhaps it is something about this combination of movement, breath and mindfulness that has a particularly strong effect on the brain.

If you wanted to put this to the test, and see whether yoga

is more than the sum of its parts, you would need to compare people who do yoga to people who practise just one of those three elements, and some researchers have been doing just that. Take for instance a small study that compared regular yoga practice to bog-standard stretching.[122] After eight weeks, older adults who were doing yoga had significant improvements in their working memory. Working memory, you'll remember, is the ability to retain small amounts of information in a very accessible way – for example, holding a new phone number in your mind while you look for a pen and paper – and it is known to help with things such as comprehension, planning and problem solving.[123] Those who did straightforward stretching saw no such improvement. In addition, the yogis ended up feeling less stressed and had lower levels of stress hormones.

Calmer brain

Another small study compared yoga to a very common form of regular light exercise: walking. People either walked or did yoga three times a week for an hour, over twelve weeks. By the end of the study those who did yoga were left with lower levels of anxiety and a greater improvement in mood than the walking

---

WHICH TYPE OF YOGA?

If you're new to yoga, trying to decide where to start can be daunting, with so many options to choose from – from the very physical to the more mindful. Science doesn't yet have all the answers, but there are some hints as to which is best depending on what you want to achieve. If you are looking to feel calmer, opt for a practice that includes poses, breathing and elements of meditation. For focus and attention, you might want to choose one that homes in on the breath. And select a more meditation-based approach, like Yin yoga, if you want to de-stress.

group.[124] This study also offered clues as to why this might be. The researchers scanned the brains of participants after their allocated exercise and found higher levels of GABA in the yogis' brains. GABA is a chemical messenger, or neurotransmitter, in the brain that plays an important role in calming down our brain activity.

Neurotransmitters like GABA are just one of many suggestions as to what might be the mechanism behind the benefits of yoga, even if we still don't truly know what is going on. Another is that yoga might heighten our mood, focus and memory by changing the activity of our brain waves. This may sound like spiritual mumbo-jumbo, but there is some evidence to back it up. Alpha brain waves are known to create greater feelings of calmness, and the size and frequency of these waves increase after yoga that involves breathing, meditation and physical poses. Breathing-based yoga, meanwhile, has the same effect on beta waves, which tend to be strongest when we are actively concentrating on a task and are linked to academic performance and arithmetic ability. A review of the available literature on the effect of practising yoga on our brain-wave activity published in 2015 concluded that 'The overall increase in brain wave activity may explain the decreases in anxiety and increases in focus that are evident after yoga training programmes.'[125]

Alternatively, yoga could be working to calm down our 'fight or flight' response, by bringing about positive changes to bodily processes involved in stress, like heart rate, blood pressure, levels of the stress hormone cortisol, and cytokines – molecules that are involved in inflammation (for more on stress, see Chapter 29).

Brain change

Perhaps the most striking explanation is that yoga can cause long-lasting changes to the structure and the function of the brain. That idea comes from brain scans of people who regularly practise yoga. When compared to people who do other types of

SCIENTIFIC SCRUTINY

The evidence is building that yoga is good for the brain, but yoga has become such a huge industry that people will promote research that doesn't stand up to scrutiny. Here's a quick checklist to see if what you read is worth taking seriously, whether it's about yoga or any scientific claim:

1. How big was the study? The bigger the better – we're talking thousands of people, rather than dozens. Diversity of participants is also important.
2. Was it published in a reputable journal, and was it peer reviewed?
3. Was there a control group in the study, against which to compare the results? So, in a study looking at the effects of yoga on the brain, was there another group of participants doing a different exercise, or nothing at all, and what happened to their brains?
4. Who funded the research, and might the funders have a vested interest in positive results?
5. Did the research involve people, or animals? (In the case of yoga, we'd assume only humans are doing the downward dog.)
6. How was the data collected – for instance, did it ask people to remember how much yoga they did in the past? How reliable is this?
7. Did the researchers take into account other factors like age, education and socioeconomic status?

exercise, the yogis had more grey matter, the part of the brain packed with brain cells and connections, in several areas of their brain, including the hippocampus. Regular meditation-based yoga in people who are very stressed can also cause shrinkage of the amygdala,[126] the area of the brain that processes fear and anxiety.

Not only do these findings help to explain why some people feel sharper after a round of sun salutations, but they also suggest that yoga might have potential as a way to stave off dementia and other age-related mental decline.

That's because grey matter in the brain diminishes as we age, and physical exercise and mindfulness practice have both been shown to be protective against this (so it makes sense yoga would too, combining as it does physical movement and meditation). Tellingly, people in the research who had more grey matter also reported fewer cognitive lapses.

So where does this leave us? Despite its ancient roots in Indian philosophy, yoga's foray into neuroscience is still young. Many of the studies so far are small, and the fact that there are so many types of yoga make it harder to study. So we do need more research to know whether it could really play a role in ageing diseases of the brain and to find out whether it can be an effective intervention to delay that decline. It's an exciting prospect though, because yoga is classed as a light exercise, which means it can be done almost anywhere, and it's modifiable too, so it is open to people of mixed physical ability and any age.

It seems fitting that despite the benefits of this holistic practice, we haven't yet been able to distil it down to the secret ingredient that makes people feel so good – we will need large, randomized control trials for that. It will also be interesting to find out whether yoga videos, rather than in-person classes, have the same effect. But if my lockdown experience is anything to go by, you don't need a fancy studio to reap the benefits – just a mat, a corner of your bedroom, and twenty minutes or so away from the demands of the day.

CHAPTER 15

Be mindful of mindfulness

From celebrity endorsements to bestselling books and hugely popular apps, meditation has become big business in recent years, in particular in the West, far from its origins as a religious or spiritual practice in East Asia.

We've already seen that yoga, which incorporates some form of meditation, can give the brain a boost, so it's perhaps not surprising that meditation on its own can be beneficial too.

There are many ways to practise meditation, and even more definitions of it, but in general you can think of it as a focusing or quietening of the mind, and one of the most ubiquitous forms is mindfulness meditation.

Mindfulness is an awareness of what's happening in your sensory experience, whether that's the feeling of your breath, the taste of your food or the sound of snow crunching under your feet. A key component is also the ability to experience those sensations without interpretation or judgement. The idea here is that we can get so caught up in our thoughts that we can't see how our thinking patterns or our emotions are affecting our behaviours. You don't need to meditate to be mindful, but it can be a helpful way to practise focusing the mind on the present moment. It is also thought that regular mindfulness meditation can help people to then be more mindful during other parts of the day too.

Fringe research

Meditation and mindfulness were fringe areas of research when scientists first turned their attention to them in the 1970s, but in the years since then a buzz has grown around the scientific claims, which exploded at the turn of the century,[127] and the Dalai Lama has even been enlisted to collaborate on research concerning the benefits of meditation to the brain.

One promising area in which the science is just catching up to what Buddhist monks have known for centuries is that mindfulness can change our perception of pain.[128]

As little as a week of mindfulness meditation training can help to lessen intensity of painful sensations, and longer practice changes how unpleasant people perceive pain to be.

Mindfulness has also been shown to help with depression and anxiety,[129] and seems to be especially promising as a way to prevent relapse in people with recurrent depression. In one study investigating the idea, more than four hundred people were given either standard antidepressants, or mindfulness-based cognitive behavioural therapy (with support to come off their antidepressants). The mindfulness therapy turned out to be as effective as the drugs, but no better.[130] That might not sound overwhelmingly successful, but when you consider that antidepressants don't work for everyone, and can cause side effects, having another equally effective option is welcome news. The treatment is now recognized by doctors in the UK as a way to prevent depression in people who have had three or more episodes of depression in the past. They are given eight weekly sessions lasting two hours each. There is also a growing movement for mindfulness to be practised by students in schools and universities.

As with yoga, meditation can change the brain, and just eight weeks of meditation practice can alter areas such as the hippocampus and amygdala, which we have seen play a crucial role in memory, fear regulation and stress, so this offers one explanation for the effects.

No panacea

Given these kinds of findings, it's no wonder that mindfulness has become such a lucrative industry. The meditation-app Headspace makes over 100 million dollars in revenue a year[131] and has more than 2 million paid subscribers.[132] Search online and you'll find claims of what meditation can do for you extending beyond depression and pain to include better focus and attention, help with problem drinking, increased happiness and a longer life, to name but a few.

Not everyone is convinced, however. Much of the research is poor quality, and it has not been conducted long enough to prove lasting effects.

Some are also uneasy about the growing popularity of meditation in the West and its role in treating mental-health problems, with too much emphasis being placed on the benefits. Speaking at a session at the Brain Forum in 2020, psychologist Miguel Farias at Coventry University, who studies, among other things, the psychological impact of meditation, pointed out that while the benefits have been fairly strong for depression and anxiety, they are more tenuous for other conditions such as eating disorders and sleep disturbances. 'We have to strike a balance between just giving drugs to our patients and on the other hand telling them that mindfulness is going to be a panacea,' he said.

Dark side

Crucially, mindfulness isn't always beneficial to the mental wellbeing of people who give it a try. Adverse effects as a consequence of meditation have been reported for decades, but research into this 'dark side' has been scant, and meditation interventions are not regulated in the same way as medicines.

HOW TO START BEING MORE MINDFUL

1. Try doing something new – it could be as small as taking a different route to work or even just sitting in a different seat than usual in your house – it might help you notice things more.
2. You might try noticing some of the everyday things you have been missing on 'autopilot' such as the sensations associated with food or the way your body feels when you walk.
3. Pick a regular time to do this, to get into the habit.
4. If you struggle with the practice, some people find it easier if there is gentle movement attached, as is the case with yoga – which we already know has many benefits.
5. Finally, if you are worried about the possible negative effects, try using a coach for face-to-face guidance.

Farias and his colleagues recently conducted a review of the existing evidence and found that around 1 in 12 people who practise meditation experience some kind of adverse effect during or after the practice,[133] and that these reactions can occur in people with no previous history of mental-health issues. Most of the research is on mindfulness in particular, and the most common adverse effects were anxiety and depression, with suicidal behaviours occurring the least frequently. To put this into context, a larger proportion – around 40 per cent – of people who take antidepressants experience some sort of side effect. Even so, this research is a warning not to assume that mindfulness is safe for everyone.

PART 4

MENTAL EXERCISE

Brain training is a multibillion-dollar industry, and growing steadily. The promise is that regularly playing computerized 'brain games' will boost your mental prowess, slow cognitive decline, make you more alert and even increase your IQ. With people living longer than ever, it's no wonder business is booming.

Sadly, the evidence for these games actually improving our brain power is less persuasive than the advertising campaigns, and results of trials have been mixed. Overall, it seems that what brain training is really good at is improving your ability to do well in brain-training games – so while it looks like you are getting a cognitive boost, the effects don't impact much on other brain areas. What's more, the time required to see these effects, years rather than months, would require an admirable level of dedication. Tellingly, activities such as crosswords and board games have been shown to give at least as good an improvement in cognition.[134]

The good news for those looking for a brain boost and ways to stave off cognitive decline is that there are other, more reliable avenues – even if they don't come with such compelling marketing campaigns. Even better, you are probably going to find them a lot more enjoyable and therefore stick to them for longer. In the following chapters, we take a look at some of the most promising.

One of these avenues is good old-fashioned learning, one of the tried and tested ways to keep dementia at bay. We'll look at why that might be, and what you can do to get the benefits.

When you're deciding what new things to learn, you'd do well to choose languages, or pick up a musical instrument. People who have done both since childhood seem to have a special kind of mental padding that protects them from damage to the brain associated with dementia. And as we discover, it is never too late to join them.

Some of this advantage may be due to neurogenesis, the hotly debated idea that adults can grow new brain cells, as we investigate in the next chapter. Whatever the brain benefits, all of these skills are likely to bring much more joy to your life than training your brain on a screen.

CHAPTER 16

You can grow new brain cells

Considering you came into this world a fairly useless creature, capable of only a handful of basic urges that amounted to little more than eating and sleeping, and unable to formulate an intelligent conscious thought, it might be shocking to consider that this version of you contained almost all the brain cells you have today. How do you go from a barely functioning being to the thoughtful, intelligent and self-aware individual who is capable of reading these words and processing their meaning? It seems incredible that you could learn so much without spawning new cells in your brain to do it with.

And yet, until relatively recently, this is exactly what people believed. Accepted wisdom has it that adult brains are simply unable to produce new cells, unlike the rest of our body, which is constantly adding, shedding and replacing bits of itself. In 1913, Spanish neuroscientist and the grandfather of neuroscience Santiago Ramón y Cajal wrote that: 'In the adult ... the nerve paths are something fixed, ended and immutable. Everything may die, nothing may be regenerated.'[135]

Instead, the growth to our brains and the learning and development we have achieved since birth were explained in large part by the formation and strengthening of connections between our brain cells, with some new brain cells appearing in childhood but none after adolescence. The number of these connections increases wildly in early childhood, which might explain why children are so scattergun in their focus and attention, and are then sculpted back through a process of pruning, keeping only the most useful connections so as to make the brain more efficient. At the same time, the brain lays down layers of insulation called myelin, which helps specific networks of neurons – or pathways – to perform better.

The first hints that we might be wrong about our ability in adulthood to produce new neurons emerged from studies in rodents that showed adults may be able to grow new neurons in the hippocampus, the brain's hub for learning and memory. Other clues came from scientists studying birdsong, who discovered that male canaries get a flurry of new neurons in their forebrains during the mating season – exactly when they have an intense period of learning new songs.[136]

What if the same thing could happen in humans? It's such an important question because it determines how we understand the influence of our environment on the brain, and challenges our thinking not just about how we learn, but also about how we might treat all kinds of neurological and psychiatric disorders in which brain cells are killed off.

Fun-house antics

To understand this, consider a famous experiment involving rodents that were either kept in standard housing or what scientists call 'enriched' housing, with plenty of opportunities to explore, play and socialize. You could think of it as a rodent theme park or holiday camp. Those living in the enriched environments displayed striking increases to the amount of new brain cells in the hippocampus, even in older individuals who had previously been living in the boring old housing. Taking old rats that had been living in an unstimulating environment, and putting them into the funfair, enabled their brains to suddenly generate a flurry of new cells in the areas vital to learning and memory.[137]

These rodents also ended up with improvements in all kinds of memory tasks.

It's easy to see, then, how the promise of a similar kind of plasticity in the human brain could be hugely beneficial not just for helping to ward off mental decline as a result of damage to brain cells, but potentially to give anyone the chance of a brain boost simply by altering their environment. If the way we live our lives could directly cause new brain cells to grow, as with those rats in the enriched cages, something that was thought to be exclusive to the young, it would completely challenge the way we understood learning to work.

Sure enough, the first strong evidence of this came in 1998, when scientists carried out post-mortems on the brains of cancer patients that had been treated with special dyes, which stain the DNA in a cell and show when it is dividing. Using this technique they were able to catch the formation of new brain cells in the act as they went through the different stages of cell division and growth (see the illustration on page 130). Specifically, they were able to spot new brain cells that were forming in the dentate gyrus, the site where memories are first formed in the brain, as well as in the hippocampus.[138] Over the following decade, some scientists began to accept that adult hippocampus neurogenesis might be possible in humans, even if some of those who did accept it believed that the ability declined sharply after middle age.

But in the last few years, two particularly promising studies suggest that there is cause for optimism that we could grow new brain cells well into old age. In 2018, Maura Boldrini at Columbia University in New York removed the brains of twenty-eight people soon after they died, ranging from fourteen to seventy-nine years of age.[139] This was the first time scientists had looked at neurogenesis in the brains of people who did not have brain disease, and so soon after death. Remarkably, her team found new brain cells in everyone they looked at, regardless of age. Those in their eighties were as capable of making new neurons as a teenager – around seven hundred a day.

A year later, scientists from Spain looked at the brains of thirteen deceased people aged from their forties to their late eighties and found signs of immature neurons in the hippocampi even in the very oldest brains. In the case of people with Alzheimer's disease, however, they found that the number of new brain cells dropped off dramatically even at the early stages of the disease, before symptoms had started and before amyloid plaques began to form. That sounds like bad news, but there is a silver lining. We've heard how efforts to treat Alzheimer's by focusing on the hallmark amyloid plaques have fared so badly, and this loss of brain cells as a possible cause of the disease could provide a new avenue for treatments.[140]

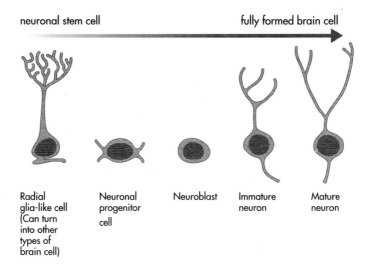

neuronal stem cell   fully formed brain cell

Radial glia-like cell (Can turn into other types of brain cell)

Neuronal progenitor cell

Neuroblast

Immature neuron

Mature neuron

The brain-cell myth

When it comes to losing brain cells, there is more good news. You might have heard the often-cited and rather depressing statistic

---

HOW TO GROW NEW NEURONS

If we truly can grow new neurons well into old age, the crucial question becomes: what can we do to grow as many as possible? The problem is that it's very hard to tell whether someone has sprouted new brain cells without slicing their brain open and having a look – most studies of neurogenesis have been done in animals or after people have died. This is not very convenient when you want to test whether a change to your daily life is having the desired effect.

Now, Dr Sandrine Thuret at King's College London and her team have developed an ingenious way to find out. They have developed what you might think of as an artificial young brain, made up of stem cells capable of turning into any type of adult cell. The team then bathe these cells in blood serum samples from people with different types of lifestyles, to see which ones encourage the growth of new cells in the artificial brain. So far they have used their test to successfully predict which people are more likely to go on to develop Alzheimer's disease. They have also been looking at the effects of diet on neurogenesis and have pinpointed twenty-two metabolites that make a difference to cognitive decline, including coffee, cocoa and fish.

---

that adults lose 1 per cent of their brain cells with each year that they age. The idea came from studies in the 1970s and 80s that appeared to show that we lose somewhere between 35 and 55 per cent of these cells during adulthood, and that this so-called 'fall out' of brain cells is what leads to mental decline. That finding has even been blamed for a rise in suicidal thoughts among the elderly during those decades, because the idea of inevitable and impeding senility was such a dispiriting one.[141]

Then, in the mid-1980s, a team of researchers scrutinizing the claim found a technical oversight in the research, leading to a radical U-turn on the subject. When researchers repeated the research taking the technical glitch into account, they found that throughout our entire adult life, we lose in total just 2 to 4 per cent of our brain cells.

This resonates with a yet more recent study of women who had made it to the impressive age of ninety or even a hundred who were found to have surprisingly large numbers of neurons in the brain, which might be connected to – or even explain – their longevity. Either way, the idea that our brain cells die off in droves as we age can be laid to rest. Of course, this doesn't change the fact that our cognitive abilities do tend to take a turn for the worse as the years wear on, but a new line of thinking is that this could be down to changes in the chemistry of the brain, or perhaps a more pronounced loss of brain cells in specific areas, including the hippocampus, one of the only areas where it now seems we can grow new ones.

If humans, like canaries, can harness the power of new brain cells to learn new tricks, not just in our youth but until our last decades, it has profound implications for the way we live our lives. The question then becomes: what can we do to nurture this intellectual regeneration? So far it seems likely that the things that trigger these new brain cells are similar to those that work for the rodents in their enriched, funfair environments. This includes – among others – things like exercise, being exposed to novelty, and socializing, and scientists are now hot on the case trying to work out exactly what works best (see the box on page 131). Eventually we may develop drugs that target this new brain cell growth directly to help with diseases of the brain and mind, or even to give anyone who wants it a memory upgrade.

On a more fundamental level, if our brain cells really can be influenced by our environments to such an extent, it just goes to show how much the way we live shapes our brains and, ultimately, who we are.[142]

CHAPTER 17

Education protects your brain

In the early 1990s, a neurologist called Yaacov Stern made a startling discovery when studying the brains of people with Alzheimer's disease. The patients all had similar symptoms, but their brains showed striking differences in the amount of damage to them. Crucially, those who were more educated had much more severe damage. Rather than conclude that education damages the brain, Stern realized that education might somehow be protecting the brains of these patients, so that despite such high levels of damage their symptoms were comparable to people whose brains were much healthier, and therefore at earlier stages of the disease.[143] The finding resonated with what had previously been seen in brain autopsies. Some people with all the signs of Alzheimer's in the brain show no symptoms at all when they are alive. Despite the damage, it never seems to affect them. Even so-called 'super agers', whose memories in their nineties are as good as those of people half their age, have been found to have such bad Alzheimer's plaques in their brains that they should have had a severe case of the disease, but somehow retained their lucidity.

Cognitive cushion

Stern's discovery that people with higher education can tolerate more damage to their brains without feeling the impact led to the idea of cognitive reserve. The thinking goes that people who were more highly educated and who had more mentally challenging jobs must have developed a kind of mental padding that protects them from the effects of the disease. This extra cushion of thinking abilities, Stern says, is a bit like a savings account – those who have built up the reserve can draw on it later when times are hard[144] – in this case, when faced with the effects of the ageing brain and neurodegenerative diseases.

There are a couple of explanations of how this might work in practice. Scans of highly educated people with Alzheimer's disease taken while they are doing cognitively difficult tasks show that they have stronger connections between different brain areas, so it looks as though they can recruit more of the brain to help them solve a mental challenge. People with a high IQ also seem to have faster brain-processing speeds, so a more efficient brain might be what's helping some people to overcome effects of dementia. Indeed, the findings now reach beyond just Alzheimer's: individuals who score more highly on tests of literacy and IQ often recover faster from stroke and head injuries, too.

To put a number on these effects, in 2006 Michael Valenzuela and Perminder Sanchev at the Prince of Wales Hospital in Sydney, Australia, conducted a review of twenty-two studies and found that people with higher education levels had a 47 per cent decreased risk of dementia. For those with a high occupational status it was 44 per cent, and those with high IQ, 42 per cent.[145] Brain scans have also revealed that people with Alzheimer's who have a higher level of education often have more amyloid build-up, adding to the idea that their brains are somehow adapting to the damage.

All this does not mean that education protects the brain against dementia itself, but it does seem to protect people from the effects of dementia. It should be said that, while many studies suggest that cognitive decline is slower in people with a higher level of education or more mentally engaging jobs, one study in 2019 looked at several thousand people with dementia and found that education didn't affect the rate of cognitive decline, nor did the researchers find signs of cognitive reserve in brain autopsies afterwards.[146] One criticism of this study is that it didn't include anyone with very low education levels, so this might be why they didn't see an effect. Or it could be that the effects of early education really do wear off with time, whereas things that continue later in life, such as a challenging job, a good social network, and sense of purpose, could be more important.

CAN YOU BOOST YOUR IQ?

If IQ really is a key to buffering the brain against cognitive decline, what can we do to increase it? To a certain extent, the power to train our intelligence is fixed by our genes – studies from twins show that about half of IQ is inherited. But that means there's still room for manoeuvre. Perhaps unsurprisingly, one way to boost your IQ is to spend more time in education. When countries increased the number of years of compulsory education, IQ increased by several points when those students had grown up. Once you're in adulthood, the best proven way to keep learning is to have a cognitively challenging job. And retire early at your peril – doing so can have a serious toll on your cognitive abilities, potentially causing enough of a drop in IQ to impact on things like financial planning. All this backs up the 'use it or lose it' hypothesis, so if you are fortunate enough to be able to stop working, don't put your feet up in front of the TV.

Further to fall

Not everyone is on board with the idea of cognitive reserve. Rather than education causing a slowing down of cognitive decline, an alternative idea is that people simply have better cognitive abilities the more education they have. If a diagnosis of dementia requires a certain threshold of cognitive impairment, these people might simply have further to fall until they get there, meaning they have a later diagnosis, even if their thinking power changes at the same rate as someone with low education levels. This idea was backed up by a review of the evidence in 2020, which found that education increases cognitive abilities across the board in adults of any age, but did not find any conclusive evidence that education slows down the actual rate at which people experience cognitive decline.[147] Yet another theory is that the brain somehow maintains more of its form and function with age in people with more education. And recent research has found that the effect of education on cognitive reserve does not seem to be uniform across people of different ethnicities, something that warrants further investigation.[148]

IQ advantage

It's also important to remember that education itself is connected to all sorts of other factors that can influence dementia risk, including the fact that educated people tend to lead healthier lives. Two recent studies have also found that IQ seems to be even more important than education. One study looked at high-school test results from thousands of people in the 1960s and compared them to their healthcare records fifty years later. It showed that low IQ increased the risk of Alzheimer's disease in both men and women by 17 per cent. Of course education itself can impact on IQ, so the two are not completely separate.[149]

Whether through cognitive reserve, IQ, or simply by increasing our cognitive abilities, it is clear that education plays a role in protecting the brain from the effects of dementia, and so, as a society, early education should be a top priority. Keeping up with mentally challenging work and hobbies well into adulthood is also imperative for keeping dementia at bay.

The bilingual brain boost

I was brought up in a bilingual household, speaking French and English, and I have always been keen to do the same for my own children. The benefits of speaking more than one language are huge, not least for the cultural aspects and the connection they can forge with other people and countries. But it is also interesting from a neurological perspective.

The idea that speaking two or even more languages is a good thing for the mind is a relatively recent one that has emerged over the last few decades. In England and many other Western countries it was thought that raising infants to be bilingual would delay their language learning and could even lead to cognitive impairments. This idea stemmed from studies in the first half of the twentieth century that found people who spoke several languages did worse on verbal tests, which were seen as a measure of cognitive ability. As one researcher famously wrote in a paper in 1929: 'bilingualism in young children is a hardship and devoid of apparent advantage'.[150]

These studies had a huge impact, but they were limited because they didn't account for lots of other important factors such as age, the socioeconomic status of families and whether a child's schooling was interrupted – something that would have been particularly relevant to immigrants and refugees. Crucially, too, the studies didn't look at proficiency in the language in which the test was administered, so poor test results were being attributed to bilingualism when it could simply have been because someone didn't understand the question.

Then, in the 1960s, Elizabeth Peal and Wallace Lambert at McGill University in Canada conducted the first study that took these factors into account. Their important paper showed that being bilingual didn't cause developmental problems at all. On the contrary, bilingual children in their study outperformed monolinguals in both verbal and non-verbal intelligence tests.[151]

Even so, it took decades for this new way of thinking to take off. However, in the last ten years or so, in part because of new scanning technologies, and also thanks to a growing understanding that our brains can physically change in response to our environment, attention has once again turned to the effects of language on the brain, and its potential to elevate the thinking mind.

Language is limitless

The innate qualities of language make this a particularly exciting prospect. There is a limit to how many hours a day you can practise the violin or contemplate the crossword. Language, on the other hand, is part of the very fabric of the human experience. Every waking moment is spent practising language in some form or other, even if just the thoughts in your head. Language also makes use of many parts of the brain at once, so any effects have the potential to go far beyond language itself, and impact on other cognitive processes and abilities, too.

Some of the first evidence of this happening came from work by Dr Ellen Bialystok, at York University in Toronto, which she conducted in the 1980s with monolingual and bilingual children. In one task the children heard a sentence and had to say whether or not it was grammatically correct. Take the phrase 'Why the dog is barking so loudly?' Both groups could easily spot that this sort of sentence was wrong. But monolingual children were also thrown by sentences that were grammatically correct but were silly or nonsensical, such as: 'Why is the cat barking so loudly?'. The bilingual children, on the other hand, had no problem with these.[152]

Bialystok suspected that the bilingual children, rather than simply demonstrating grammatical know-how, were in fact displaying a stronger ability in what we call executive control, or executive function. The brain's executive system is a broad range of mental skills that help us to carry out desired behaviours, allowing us to focus on the task at hand and block out irrelevant information. In this case, the bilingual children were able to ignore the irrelevant fact of whether the sentence was silly and focus solely on the grammar.

Another sign of executive function is to be able to switch easily between one task and another, and this is also something bilinguals have been shown to be good at – for example, switching easily between categorizing things by shape or colour without making mistakes.[153]

Constant workout

What is it about language that affords the brain this cognitive fine-tuning? One explanation is that when we know more than one language, the brain has to constantly suppress the words of the language we don't wish to use at the same time as selecting the words or the meanings from the desired language. It's as if the brain is conducting a constant workout, exercising its executive control with every word.

More recently, Bialystok has argued that the explanation is to do with the way in which bilingualism accelerates the development and maintenance of attention. The bilingual experience seems to adapt brain systems to make them better at paying attention to the right element of a task, she says. From an early age, the demands of bilingualism may fine-tune this system of executive attention, which results in cognitive benefits throughout life. This could explain the wide range of effects that have been noted in bilinguals, but none has caused such a stir as the finding that the mental benefits of language learning could extend into old age, and possibly delay the onset of dementia.

Back in 2007, Bialystok and her team were studying a group of people with dementia in a memory clinic in Toronto, half of whom were bilingual. They found that the bilingual group experienced the first symptoms of dementia on average 4.1 years later than the monolinguals. When they repeated the study for people specifically with Alzheimer's disease, the effect was even greater, with bilinguals experiencing the onset of symptoms about five years later.[154]

After these initial findings, there was understandably a lot of excitement about the prospect of delaying dementia simply by speaking another language. The thinking goes that this constant switching that bilinguals do between one language and the other, and the brain workout it gives them, contributes to cognitive reserve, which as we saw in the previous chapter is a sort of mental cushion that protects people from the detrimental effects of ageing on the brain.[155]

Disappointingly, however, several scientists have more recently tried to replicate Bialystok's study and failed to get the same results. This has led to a heated debate about the brain-boosting abilities of bilingualism, and whether we should believe the hype.

Why might it be that the results didn't hold true in the other studies? One big issue is the same thing that makes language so promising as a brain-booster: it's so deeply interconnected to everything we do. As we've seen with other lifestyle factors such as exercise, it can be hard to separate out one part of a person's lifestyle from another. In the case of bilingualism research, many of the findings, including those from Bialystok's group, which is based in Canada, were conducted in Western populations,

---

LEARNING A LANGUAGE

We know that a second language is good for the brain, but what are the best ways to go about learning one?

1. Do it because you want to. How motivated people feel about learning a new language can predict how well they do, so find one you feel passionate about learning.
2. Sleep on it. The brain shifts our memories into long-term storage while we sleep, so learning before you go to bed is a good idea. Even a nap after studying can help.
3. Mix new vocabulary in gradually. The brain seeks out new information, and mixing new material in with older information is a proven way to help you remember more.
4. It's never too late. One study looking at the age at which immigrants learned a new language found there was no critical cut-off after childhood. Anyone can learn, although success decreases gradually with age.

---

where often the bilinguals were also immigrants. There might have been something special about this fact that was responsible for the bilingual brain boost: perhaps those immigrants who successfully made it to their new home and managed to set up a new life for themselves were already more resilient in other ways. Another factor that might play a role is education, or even general intelligence. Could it be that people who are better educated or smarter go on to learn more languages? After all, as we just saw, education has been shown in several studies to delay the onset of dementia.

A different kind of bilingual

Although it may not seem like it to those of us who have been brought up in largely monolingual societies, at least half of the world speaks more than one language. In India, most people speak several and, fortunately for our purposes, being bilingual is not tied to immigration or even education and socioeconomic status. Even illiterate people can speak many languages.

Taking advantage of this situation, Dr Thomas Bak, a cognitive neuroscientist at the University of Edinburgh in Scotland, and Dr Suvana Alladi, who was working on memory disorders at Nizam's Institute of Medical Sciences in Hyderabad in India, teamed up to see whether they found any effects of language on dementia. Strikingly, when they looked at about six hundred people who had come into the clinic for dementia, they found that bilinguals had symptoms that started around four and a

---

HOW PROFICIENT DO YOU HAVE TO BE?

We often think of bilinguals as people who learned from childhood or speak faultlessly, but while scientists are still working out the details on just how good you need to be at languages to get the bilingual advantage, there's good news for all of us.

1. You can learn later in life. Recent research looking at adults who learned a language as part of a degree course found that they scored better in tasks of executive control than monolinguals. Even a one-week language course can produce some long-lasting benefits, as long as people keep practising for at least five hours a week.

2. You can speak 'Franglais'. Good news for families who switch between languages constantly – sometimes even in the same sentence. Mixing up languages like this can still confer cognitive advantages.

3. More languages don't necessarily mean a bigger boost. Tentative findings suggest no benefit to speaking more than two languages. This fits with the theory that any boost comes from the mental gymnastics involved in constantly switching between languages, and two languages should be enough for that.

half years later than monolinguals[156] – almost exactly the same finding as Bialystok's work in Toronto.

Evidence from brain scans is also adding to the picture that bilingualism does work. Bilingual brains have more white and grey matter in areas involved in cognitive processing, and scans of people with probable Alzheimer's disease in Toronto were found to have more damage in several brain areas associated with the disease and yet had similar cognitive abilities to monolinguals, suggesting that bilingualism can build cognitive reserve and protect against the effects of disease, just as with those people who have higher levels of education whom we heard about in the last chapter. There is some evidence that bilingual people with Alzheimer's might also have lower levels of tau proteins in the brain than monolinguals – one of the key proteins implicated in Alzheimer's disease.

What researchers are realizing from all this is that it is likely there are many brain benefits from speaking more than one language, and that these are especially marked late in life – not least a delay to the onset of dementia. That said, language is messy. Not only is it tied in with other factors, such as education and intelligence, but speaking a language isn't all or nothing. Some people use one language at home and another at work or school, whereas others switch between languages all the time. This complexity has left some researchers thinking about language in the same way that we consider a healthy diet. We know the Mediterranean diet is good for us, but there's no point in focusing too much on whether it's the olive oil or the fish that's doing the work. Similarly, language might be more than the sum of its parts. Rather than focus on exactly the right way to do it, if you enjoy languages, then learning a new one will only bring benefits. And teaching them to children can be a fun way for us all to learn. So enjoy it and any health benefits that come with it, too.

CHAPTER 19

Music should be part of daily life

In his 1871 book *The Descent of Man*, Charles Darwin famously mused on what might be the point of music, declaring that 'neither the enjoyment nor the capacity of producing musical notes are faculties of the least use to man in reference to his daily habits of life …' As we shall discover in this chapter, he couldn't have been more wrong.

The power of music

Let's start with the 'capacity of producing musical notes', as Darwin put it, or more simply, the ability to play music. Musical training is multisensory and draws together lots of different cognitive abilities and brain areas. Not only do musicians need to be able to read, listen to, understand and perform the music; they need excellent perceptual processing[157] to interpret sounds and rhythm. And to play an instrument you need fine motor skills too. It's probably because the brain workout you get from music is so widespread – coupled with the fact that learning music requires regular practice – that music training seems to have an impact not just on abilities related to musicality but also on more general cognitive abilities. Musicians have been found to have improvements in executive functions including working memory, as well as spatial, mathematical and non-verbal abilities. They have structural changes to their brains, too, and a study from

2021, the largest of its kind, showed that musicians have stronger connections between different brain areas, and that those areas talk to each other more, than in people who don't practise music.

Could it be that there is something special about the brains of these people that predisposes them to being good at music and could also explain this cognitive advantage? Or is it truly down to music itself? To try and unravel the question, an international team of researchers from the Netherlands, Denmark and Finland ran a battery of intelligence and executive function tests on 101 adults in Finland and grouped them according to their musical expertise – non-musicians, amateurs and musicians.[158] They also took into account their socioeconomic status, personality traits and other factors that could influence the results. Even after controlling for all these, the musicians did better in the cognitive tests, and the more musical training they had, the better they scored: the professional musicians were better than amateurs, who were in turn better than the non-musicians. The study authors believe that music lessons train our all-important executive functions, which we know benefit almost all cognitive abilities.

How young do you have to start? You may have heard of the Mozart effect: the belief that listening to classical music could lead to a direct boost in children's IQ. What really seems to be going on, however, is simply that music can boost mood and arousal, and a better mood is conducive to improved learning, which in turn can help you do a bit better on an IQ test. That's not to say the effect isn't useful, even if it has nothing directly to do with Mozart. In the same way that a burst of exercise can help children focus and do better in school (see Chapter 12), a music break could also help cognitive performance directly afterwards.

Learning to play music at a young age is even more powerful: it has been linked with general intelligence in children, and several studies show that those who learn music experience a boost to IQ, compared to those who practise something else instead, like drama. A recent study of 100 children aged around nine years old found that those who practised a musical instrument for at least half an hour a week did better on general intelligence tests and also had an increase in white matter in the brain, which is a kind of insulation that helps the brain send signals more efficiently. The more practice the children did, the more of these changes they had in the brain.[159] But don't panic if you learned an instrument as a child, then gave up: the effects on memory and IQ might even last into adulthood, one study found. But music is like education – the more you learn, the stronger the effects.[160]

OPERA HYPOTHESIS

Increasingly, evidence shows that musical training can improve our ability to process speech, too, for instance picking out speech accurately from noise. According to a popular explanation, called the Opera hypothesis, put forward by Aniruddh Patel at Tufts University, Massachusetts, music and speech share some of the same cognitive processing areas in the brain, but music is more taxing, and also brings in emotion and the need for focused attention. This gives these systems such a good workout that the brain permanently changes in structure and function, so that speech processing is easier. This is good news for anyone who regularly practises music, but it might also offer ways to help people with hearing difficulties, something that researchers are already investigating.

To get the biggest cognitive boost from music, starting young and lots of practice is the winning formula, it seems. But all is not lost if you are late to the game, according to a study of adults with no prior musical experience who had piano lessons for six months and improved on tests of executive functions.[161]

The fact that music is so good for our thinking skills has attracted interest from scientists curious to know whether all these broad improvements in the brain might endow musicians with the same mental cushioning that we see in linguists.

So far, the evidence is promising. A five-year study of almost five hundred older people who didn't have dementia at the start of the study found that playing a musical instrument was one of several leisure activities that reduced their dementia risk (the others were reading, playing card games and dancing).[162] Further evidence comes from pairs of twins in which one sibling is musical and the other isn't, with the musician in the pair on average 64 per cent less likely to develop dementia.[163] And research from 2021 shows that older adults with a musical training had larger volumes of brain areas important for executive function, memory, learning and emotion.[164] All this goes to show that having a musical bent should set you up well for a suite of long-term cognitive benefits, even if the field has had a lot less research than language.[165] The next step will be to see whether older people might be able to train their brains in order to stave off cognitive decline with regular music practice, and research is already underway to find out.[166]

Healing rhythm

So now let's turn to the enjoyment of music, which Darwin also believed held no value for daily life. Here, too, he was way off the mark. One group of people who can benefit tremendously from listening to music is those with neurological disorders. In people with dementia, for instance, listening to music can improve mood and behaviour long after the tune has stopped.[167]

According to Professor Psyche Loui at Northeastern University, in Boston, Massachusetts, who studies the effect of music on the brain, there are certain frequencies of brain activity that are linked to cognition. These rhythmic patterns of brain activity are triggered when we are mentally focused on something, but they degrade in older age, especially in neurodegenerative diseases. So it might be that the rhythmic element of music could be reinvigorating these frequencies in people with cognitive problems, giving them more mental clarity.

This got Loui wondering whether it might be possible to design music that turbocharges our ability to concentrate, and she has now joined forces with a start-up called brain.fm – which makes music to help people focus – to find out. They have been cooking up new music from scratch, using the elements of music almost like an ingredients list, and have found that inserting certain frequencies of sound causes the brain to lock into those frequencies, helping people to concentrate for longer and do better on cognitive tests that require sustained attention. With this music in their ears, people feel like they want to plough on with their work rather than get distracted by social media and other temptations, Loui says, and this seems to be particularly useful for those who report some ADHD-like tendencies – people who lose focus easily.

Frequency aside, Loui also believes that the predictive nature of music can be especially beneficial to those with neurological disorders, in particular Parkinson's disease, a gradual disorder of the nervous system that usually causes movement problems such as stiffness and tremors.

Brain at rest   Brain reacting to music

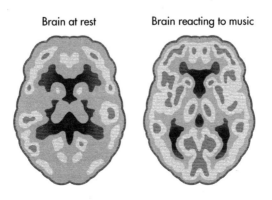

BACKGROUND NOISE

Aside from music, other sounds can mess with our mental performance. Studies have found that specific noises have the power to interfere with learning – for instance, children attending school under flight paths tend to lag behind their peers and find it harder to stick with problems. And people – including children – are especially easily distracted by the sound of babble, or background speech. But there are ways to turn background noise to your advantage: get the volume right and it could give you a creative boost. One experiment tested a range of noises on people's creativity and found that the type of sound didn't matter, but it shouldn't be too soft or too loud – probably because that volume heightens your arousal levels just the right amount.

Most music is predictive in that, after we hear a few beats of a tune, our brain anticipates what's going to come next. To make these predictions, rhythm gets different parts of the brain talking to each other, which helps us anticipate the next part of the tune. What's more, rhythm is processed in the motor parts of the brain, even when we are not moving. One of the issues with Parkinson's disease is that the motor system has a hard time initiating movement, but by listening to music and switching on this brain-wide reaction to rhythm, Loui thinks we can prime the brain's motor system to be ready to initiate movement more easily. It's as if our intrinsic affinity for rhythm is using the connection with the auditory system to kick-start movement in brain areas that are degenerated in Parkinson's.

Loui's recent research backs this up, and last year her team published research showing that just four months of weekly dance classes improves both motor and non-motor symptoms of Parkinson's disease. Intriguingly, the biggest improvement seen was in those who had prior dance experience, possibly because they already had this strong connection between the auditory and motor systems.[168] To take this idea one step further, Loui and her team are now working with a company called Oscilloscope to see whether rhythmic flashes of light that mimic musical rhythm might help to restore these connections in the brain directly.[169]

The predictive nature of music also seems to help people in nursing homes who can become agitated, especially those with dementia – which can be a struggle for carers. Part of the reason people with neurodegenerative disorders get agitated is that their memory loss diminishes their ability to predict what's going to happen in the future, which can be disorientating. Because music instantly gets the brain making predictions, it can have this calming and comforting effect.

Musical interlude

The rest of us can benefit from the ability of a good tune to improve brain power, but the playlist you choose will matter. Listening to music taps into the same feel-good reward systems in the brain that are activated by sex, great food or money. But this only happens when you listen to music of your choice. That reward activation is probably also linked to the predictive nature of music – being able to accurately forecast what comes next gives your brain a buzz. Loui has found that if people regularly listen to music they love, after eight weeks this connection between the auditory and reward systems in the brain is strengthened. Aside from making people feel good, this can have unexpected benefits – the study participants also report feeling less lonely, and less stressed, during the music intervention. Loui hopes that this could become a simple and long-term lifestyle choice that midlife adults could adopt to help reduce feelings of stress and loneliness as they age.

All this goes to show quite how wrong Darwin was in his dismissal of music. Practising music from an early age and throughout your life, or other kinds of musical training, can change the shape of the brain, improve cognition and potentially protect against dementia in a similar way to languages. But even those of us who have zero musical talent can still improve our brain through music. Simply listening to music gives the brain a workout, so maybe we should consider tuning in to a favourite playlist in the same way as we view a healthy diet and regular exercise – as something we should build into our daily habits for a long-term boost to mental wellbeing. If ever you needed an excuse to break from work and crank up the music, this is it.

FOUR MUSICAL LIFE HACKS

1. Going into hospital? Take some headphones. Listening to music before, during and after surgery can reduce pain and anxiety, and the amount of drugs needed.
2. If a family road trip is on the cards, ban headphones and turn up the car stereo. Research shows that listening to music with your children can lead to better relationships with them in young adulthood.
3. Dancing to 'groovy' music can get you into a state of flow. Even scientists use the term 'groovy' to describe music that almost everyone wants to dance to, and this kind of tune in particular elicits a state of flow that has been linked to improvements in levels of anxiety and self-esteem.
4. To feel happier, listen to happy music. Listening regularly over two weeks has been found to boost people's mood, especially when they were specifically told to try and use the music to this end – the intention itself played a part.

PART 5

SOCIAL LIFE

As much as we can all take steps to improve our mental health and abilities, we are not alone in this endeavour. We do not live in a vacuum, and our interactions with others – or lack thereof – can also profoundly influence our brain health and happiness. Humans are sociable creatures by nature, and we evolved to be part of an interconnected social network. It's only a small step to see, then, why having rich and meaningful connections is so good for the brain, and why loneliness can be bad news for our grey matter. A growing number of us are living on our own, but as we discover in Chapter 21, this doesn't necessarily make us lonelier.

For those who do live with others, those relationships – especially marriage – can be a boon to our mental health, given the right circumstances (see Chapter 20). The same goes for our four-legged friends (or, in some cases, more unusual pets), as we explore in Chapter 22.

Finally, our social lives don't just include our companions, but also have a strong interplay with our environment. How much time we spend indoors versus outside, at what time of the day or night, and whether our social activities take place surrounded by nature, can all have a profound effect on our mental wellbeing, as we discover in the final two chapters of this section. So let's take a look at how to harness the power of our relationships and environment to make us feel better, and think smarter.

CHAPTER 20

Marriage can protect you from dementia

Some do it for love, others for money or simply just out of tradition. But whatever the reason, getting married can do wonders for your health. Married people tend to live longer, have better cardiovascular health and lower blood pressure – with some studies showing men benefit more than women from these health effects.

Given the benefits to the body, scientists began to wonder whether marriage might also have an impact on mental health as we get older. So in 2017, an international team of scientists scoured the literature and pooled together the results from all the studies they could find looking at the mental benefits of long-term partnerships. In total, their research included fifteen studies, with over eight hundred thousand participants, that looked at the effect of marriage on dementia. They found that compared to those who are married, single and widowed people are at a higher risk of developing the condition – single people have around a 40 per cent higher, and widowed people a 20 per cent higher risk of dementia than those who are married, even after taking into account age and gender. [170] Interestingly, the study didn't show any higher risk among those who have been divorced, which is surprising given that this can be such a difficult experience, and that stress itself has been linked to dementia risk.

There are a number of reasons why tying the knot could delay dementia. The first is that being married generally results in daily social interaction, which, as we'll see in the next chapter, is good for the mind. Keeping socially active might also increase cognitive reserve – that mental buffer that seems to protect us from the effects of damage to the brain as we age.

An even simpler explanation is that people who are married have healthier lifestyles on the whole,[171] which is also good for the grey stuff. This probably isn't the complete answer though, because although being healthy helps you live longer, in the research the effects of matrimony against dementia were even greater than the impact on longevity. This implies that marriage has some kind of direct impact on the brain, rather than simply improving our physical health and, by consequence, the mind too. The researchers behind the study think that it's a lifetime of cohabitation that drives up cognitive reserve – that the social interaction is the most important thing. We don't have to limit it just to those who are married. The research used the institution of marriage as a proxy for being in a long-term relationship, and included studies that mentioned a partner, not just a spouse.

Losing a loved one

Why are people who are widowed at higher risk of dementia, but not those who get divorced? Previous studies have shown that widowhood is more stressful than divorce, in general, so it could be the stress of losing a loved one that's causing the increase in dementia risk.

Single people are more likely to go undiagnosed for dementia, possibly because it's harder to pick up in those who attend a clinic alone, and because partners and spouses are the most likely to notice early signs that their loved one is becoming more forgetful or experiencing changes in their behaviour. So, it might be particularly important for doctors to take special notice when their patients don't have a significant other in their lives.

Overall, then, coupling-up sounds like a good idea if you want to lower your dementia risk. Of course, not all relationships are made of the same stuff. The quality of a marriage – that is to say, how satisfied people are with it – also comes into play. To measure this, scientists use questionnaires[172] that probe people about niggly issues such as how much they and their spouse disagree on dealing with the in-laws, or how they display affection, as well as bigger questions, like whether they would marry someone else if they could live their life over again. Research using this approach shows that it's not marriage per se that confers a range of benefits, including a lower risk of depression, more happiness, lower stress levels, and greater life satisfaction than single people. Instead, it's the contentment and the support associated with the relationship that's important. If the marriage is good, it can boost mental health, but research says you're better off being single than in an unhappy marriage.[173]

Special someone

Marriages (and presumably other long-term, committed relationships) do have something special, though. You might think that if you are single or in a bad marriage, the downsides of that to your health could be countered by a great bunch of friends who step in to fill that social void. But other social networks, however strong or extensive, are unable to protect people from the mental drawbacks of an unhappy marriage or from being single. A single person with a great support network is still likely to be worse off than someone in a happy marriage, and those in a bad marriage can't undo the negative effects on mental health by having that outside support. This may be due to the unrivalled level of commitment, or the intimacy of the relationship, although it's too soon in this new area of research to say for sure.

While we are on the subject of intimacy, there might be another way that being in a relationship helps the brain: sex.

HOW MANY CHILDREN WILL MAKE YOU HAPPIEST?

For those who become parents, a big question is deciding when to stop. What can science tell us about how many children will make us happiest? Some clues come from a study by sociologist Hans-Peter Kohler at the University of Pennsylvania, who sent a questionnaire to identical twins in Denmark taking part in a national twin survey, and who had gone on to have children (using identical twins ruled out lots of other factors that could influence happiness). He found that both men and women became happier with the birth of their first child, although having a son played a big part for men, who claimed to feel 75 per cent happier when they had a son compared to having a daughter. On the arrival of a second child, the fathers saw negligible change to their happiness, while the mothers' happiness decreased, implying that for ultimate happiness, one is the magic number. But research on people becoming parents in Germany and Britain paints a different picture. It found that happiness increases with the first and the second child, but not the third, suggesting you should stop at two. Why the disparity? Clearly, other things play a part, and studies show that how happy having children makes you depends on factors like living in a developed country, your age – those over thirty were happier when they became parents – as well as being well-off and having a good education. Whether the number of children you have matches how many you hoped to have is also important.

Older people who engage in regular sexual activity score better on tests of cognitive ability, particularly aspects involved in working memory and executive function. [174] This is possibly due to the burst of the reward chemical dopamine released during sex, as dopamine is known to help with these kinds of cognitive abilities in older people.

As for having children, even people in committed relationships have long been reported to experience a dip in mental wellbeing when they have children, attributed to lack of sleep, money and time. That picture has shifted a bit in the last couple of years, however, with new research showing that it's not having children that makes people unhappy; it's the financial cost.[175] Take money out of the equation and parents are considerably happier. How many children also matters (see the box opposite). What's more, once kids leave home, parents do end up happier than those who remained child free.[176] Empty-nesters benefit from the rich and meaningful family connection they get from being parents, as well as support into old age (if they are lucky) – without the childcare burden they had to deal with when their children were young.

CHAPTER 21

How loneliness changes your brain

In 2020, as much of the world went into lockdown in response to the coronavirus pandemic, a different health issue was also propelled into the spotlight: loneliness. A search of the medical research repository Pubmed shows that there were double the number of scientific papers published on loneliness and mental health in 2020 compared to the previous year. But while some of these studies have found an increase in reports of loneliness during that time, and alongside that an increase in depression and even suicidal thoughts, even in relatively young people, other studies came to the opposite conclusion: that people felt 'in it together' during the pandemic, that they perceived themselves to be connected in other ways, sometimes even more connected to others than they were before the pandemic.[177]

These findings show just how complicated the question of loneliness is, and the pandemic only adds to a growing concern in recent years over the physical and mental-health impacts of loneliness – an issue that has led to a proliferation of headlines proclaiming an 'epidemic of loneliness'. The number of people living alone is increasing, these articles argue, and therefore so is the number of people feeling lonely.

Worse than smoking?

Why does it matter? One of the most often-cited notions about the effect of loneliness is that it will send us to an early grave, and that being lonely is worse for us than obesity or smoking. In 2018, the UK government declared that 'Loneliness is one of the greatest public health challenges of our time', listing effects on health including heart disease, stroke and Alzheimer's disease, and pledged a whole raft of new strategies to try and combat this plight. These include postal workers checking up on people who are socially isolated, and a plan for doctors to be able to refer lonely patients to community activities or volunteering services. The country even has a dedicated 'loneliness minister'.

It's not hard to see why social isolation may be bad for us – having strong social networks is more likely to see us having access to a job, healthier food and physical activity. Loneliness can also decrease willpower, which might lead us to make less healthy choices.

But we would be mistaken to think of social isolation as a proxy for loneliness.

The problem is that we tend to conflate the issue of being lonely with that of being alone, but as you have probably experienced at some point in your life, it's perfectly possible to feel lonely even when surrounded by others, and feel at peace when we are on our own. Intuitively, then, we know that being alone and being lonely aren't the same thing, and the data concur.

As an example, let's look to Denmark and Sweden, two of the countries globally with the highest proportion of people living on their own. Compared to other countries in Northern Europe, people there report relatively low levels of loneliness. Only around a quarter of people surveyed in Denmark and Sweden report feeling lonely at least some of the time, compared to 62 per cent in Greece, the country that topped the charts for loneliness.[178] So spending time alone is clearly not a good predictor of whether we feel lonely or lack social support.

In 2012, researchers Caitlin Coyle and Elizabeth Dugan, at the University of Massachusetts, Boston, set out to examine the relationship between social isolation, loneliness and mental health in more detail. Their study of almost 1,200 people found a very weak connection between social isolation and loneliness. Put another way, just because someone is on their own, don't assume they are lonely, and don't assume that people who are lonely are socially isolated. What the two researchers did find was a strong link between loneliness and poor mental health.[179]

So we need to remember that loneliness is actually the perception, the sensation, of feeling isolated – even if we have lots of people around. It's about how our social expectations match up to the reality.

THE LONELIEST YEARS

Reframing how we think of loneliness as a perception of social isolation is important because, as a society, we tend to assume that those who are alone are those who are most at risk. Many of us assume, for instance, that loneliness is a plight of the elderly. In fact, young people in rich countries are more likely to report feeling lonely than older people. Loneliness then tends to decrease in middle age, before peaking again after the age of seventy-five. This means we should not think about loneliness equating with older age, and should include policies and provisions for younger people to cope with loneliness. However, even if young people do feel lonely, they don't seem to be any lonelier than young people were in the past, so it would be wrong to say that they are getting lonelier. The same is true for older individuals – just because there are more people than ever living on their own, it doesn't mean we have an epidemic of loneliness.

Evolved to feel lonely

To understand why this subjective experience of loneliness can be so bad for us, especially for the brain, it helps to think about what purpose feelings of loneliness may serve. That awful sensation in fact has an evolutionary purpose. We are a social species, and evolved to live in groups for survival, so it would be advantageous for our ancestors to feel bad when they ended up on their own. The late John Cacioppo, a researcher at the University of Chicago, who studied loneliness for decades, called it a biological warning system similar to hunger and thirst.[180] That unpleasant feeling tells us we should quickly return to the fold for our own safety. This explanation also fits with studies that Cacioppo and others performed, looking at the immune system. People who are socially isolated have an overactive inflammatory response, part of the immune system that kicks in to protect us from pathogens, say from a wound. It seems that when we are on our own, the body is priming itself for an impending attack. Keep that going for too long and we are heading for trouble, seeing as too much inflammation can start to cause damage to tissues and organs, and has been implicated in numerous physical and mental-health conditions. Loneliness has certainly been found to increase the risk of mental-health problems, such as depression, anxiety and stress.[181]

Either way, for people who are chronically lonely, this becomes a problem because their body doesn't shift back out of this survival mode, and is constantly primed for an attack.

As well as causing health problems that come with sustained inflammation, loneliness also changes the brain, making it hyper-vigilant. It's as if lonely people are constantly on the lookout for threats, especially in a social context. This bias towards the negative also affects how they view relationships, making them more likely to interpret negative intent in people's actions, to adopt protective behaviours that mean they are less likely to put themselves out there, and more prone to expect rejection.[182] Not only are all these things bad for our mental health, but they also put people at risk of social withdrawal, compounded by the fact that inflammation leaves us less motivated to seek out the company of others. All of which can create a vicious spiral of loneliness that may be hard to break. Loneliness often causes sleep issues, too, which can also be explained by this hyper-vigilance stopping people from switching off. And possibly related to sleep issues, loneliness is linked to impaired executive function, accelerated cognitive decline[183] and progression towards Alzheimer's disease.[184]

A CURE FOR LONELINESS?

With loneliness billed as a major health emergency that can have a dire effect on both our physical and emotional wellbeing, some researchers are wondering whether it could be cured like other ailments – with a pill. Professor Stephanie Cacioppo, John Cacioppo's widow and a neuroscientist also at the University of Chicago, is running a clinical trial of a hormone called pregnenolone, which has been shown to help in animal studies with the kind of anxiety and exaggerated fear responses associated with loneliness. Others are exploring the use of oxytocin, often referred to as the 'cuddle chemical' because it can increase pro-social behaviour and trust in people. The results of these trials are imminent, and the idea is that a drug could help people break the cycle of negative thoughts and behaviours that can accompany loneliness, in conjunction with other treatments such as cognitive behavioural therapy. But not everyone is convinced that medicating against loneliness is the way to go.

Perceived loneliness

If loneliness is so bad for our brains, what can we do to protect against it? Part of the answer is understanding what causes it in the first place. Building on the idea that loneliness is about the perception of isolation, rather than actual social isolation, and a mismatch about what we expect versus that reality, a 2018 survey of more than six thousand people in the US found that it was those people who were more dissatisfied with their family life, social life or local community who were much more likely to feel lonely.[185] So if you aren't satisfied with your social circle, you are at risk of loneliness and should take steps to make a change.

For older people, health is another factor – those who rate their health as good are less likely to report feeling lonely, probably because health problems keep people from doing the social activities they would like. So focusing on those health issues as the root cause is important.

For younger people in particular, that mismatch can come from a lack of romantic relationships, or moving to a new city without a social network. Again, it's not being alone that's the issue here; it's being alone when you don't want to be. Genetics also seems to play a part in why some people end up feeling lonely in situations that someone else would not. Ultimately, we all need different amounts of social contact, so listen to that feeling inside and act on it if you start to feel lonely.

FEELING WARM AND FUZZY

Feeling lonely? Take a warm bath. When we talk about a warm person, we imagine someone kind who makes us feel good. That idea of personal warmth also translates through physical sensations. People are more likely to be nice to others after holding a warm drink, for instance. Holding something warm can also lessen the negative impact of thinking about a time when we were socially excluded. We can make use of this for loneliness, too – taking a warm bath appears to help people feel less lonely, presumably by unconsciously substituting some of that interpersonal warmth they crave with the physical sensation.

FIVE SIMPLE WAYS TO PROTECT AGAINST LONELINESS

1. Make time for your besties. We've evolved to have a very small inner circle of friends, and according to evolutionary psychologist Professor Robin Dunbar, you need to dedicate 40 per cent of your efforts on those five or so people to maintain a meaningful, rather than a large, social network.

2. Think of your relationships like a diet. For a satisfying meal, try and get your social calories from a mix of sources – intense close friendships as well as those small interactions such as talking to the person at the checkout. They all add up.

3. Find a sense of purpose, especially something that involves other people.

4. Why not volunteer for a loneliness charity – not only will it help you with that all-important sense of purpose; you could also bring others out of loneliness, too.

5. Remember that loneliness can happen to anyone, old or young, and it messes with your brain – making you doubt other people's intentions. Keep that in mind when loneliness strikes to try and break the cycle.

Of course, we can't always avoid moving to a new city, or ending up single when we want to be in love, but even then there are things we can do to try and avoid the loneliness trap. One trick is to focus less on the quantity of social connections you have, and more on the quality of those relationships. If you can't see people in person as often as you'd like (hello, 2020), by all means use social media to stay in touch, but avoid passively scrolling – this has been shown to make people feel worse than using these apps to actually connect with people. And try to cut down on the number of people you follow but don't know, focusing instead on your real-life friends.

If you are stuck in a rut of serious loneliness though, the best thing to do is to seek out some cognitive behavioural therapy that will challenge those negative thought patterns and break the spiral. One review by John Cacioppo and his colleagues that looked at all sorts of interventions against loneliness, including things such as improving people's social skills and enhancing their social support, found that addressing this so-called 'maladaptive social cognition', the negative thoughts that come with hyper-vigilance, was the most successful.[186]

Another way to break the loneliness cycle and shake off those negative self-thoughts is to find something that gives you purpose,[187] whether that's through helping others like volunteering, career goals or education, joining a choir, or starting a new hobby.

CHAPTER 22

The healing power of pets

The story of Hiro is a familiar one to many of us who have moved into a bustling metropolis. Arriving in Tokyo from his hometown of Nagoya, leaving behind his girlfriend and family in order to take on a demanding job, it didn't take long for the young man to become socially isolated. After a couple of years, this had led to feelings of depression, and anxiety over his financial situation. 'Other than work I didn't see anyone, I was sleeping too much, and was always alone at home,' he recalls. But this is where Hiro's story takes an unusual turn. To deal with these feelings, he did not seek out a therapist, or take on a hobby to meet likeminded people. Instead, he started visiting a cat cafe. 'I just thought that if I could play with cats, I would be able to be energetic again,' he says.[188]

If you already share your life with a furry friend, you'll be able to empathize with the idea that seeking out what Hiro calls 'skinship', or physical contact, from an animal can lift your mood. On top of the cuddles, pets provide company, a sense of purpose and, of course, unconditional love.

There is now huge interest in whether all this might add up to a tangible boost to both our physical and mental health. This idea really took off in the 1980s with studies on the health benefits of owning a pet, in particular helping with allergies and improving cardiovascular and psychological health. Not for lack of trying, however, attempts to replicate these studies are often unsuccessful. One explanation is that some of the physical health effects can be explained by social factors – for instance, research has found that people who own a pet are also more likely to own their own house. This suggests they might be better off, and as a result have access to other resources that account for the health improvement.

Things are a bit more promising when it comes to mental wellbeing. One idea here is that pets, especially dogs, can improve mental health by indirect means. For instance, they are a wonderful catalyst for social interactions, and we've already heard how important a strong social network is for the mind. Dog owners often become friendly with other dog owners in their local park, which can be a particular boon to those who are at risk of social isolation, such as older people and those with disabilities. Getting out for daily walks also helps tick off many of the other brain-boosting behaviours covered elsewhere in this book – spending time in nature, exposure to daylight, getting fresh air, and of course regular exercise. Being forced out of the house by a dog desperate for a walk (and possibly being forced to interact with others too) could be especially important for people with depressive symptoms that can lead to a vicious cycle of isolation and low mood. Pets are also more likely to encourage people into a routine, which can similarly have a positive impact on mental health.

Social support

Human relationships help protect our mental health by offering emotional support, reducing the perception of stressful events (amazing how going for drinks with friends can de-escalate a stressful day and put things into perspective) and protecting from anxiety-related illness. Strong social bonds also help people recover faster from illness. All this amounts to what we call social support, and a dearth of it can be as bad for our health as smoking, obesity or a lack of physical exercise.[189] It might be a stretch to say that your pet offers emotional support, but it does offer companionship, and this has been proven to mirror some of the same elements of human relationships that improve our health. For instance, pets have been shown to help in the early stages of bereavement.

The effects of pet ownership on our brain might also mimic those of human connections. One small study looked at women's brains in an MRI scanner when they viewed pictures of their dog and of their child, and found that both images activated some of the same areas involved in emotion, reward, affiliation and social cognition. The women also rated the pictures as eliciting similar amounts of pleasantness and arousal, although there were other differences too – the brain responses for emotion, reward and affiliation were stronger when they looked at their baby, compared to more activity in areas of the brain related to visual processing of faces and social cognition when they looked at their dog.[190] Still, this might help to explain why some people go so far as to treat their pet much like they would an actual baby, and feel that connection so strongly.

Prison pooch

Such is the promise of animals to help people's mental health that they have now been trialled in all sorts of settings. One pilot study by the Centre for Mental Health in the UK set out to see whether dogs could help tackle the rising numbers of suicides and self-harm in prisons. The team brought in therapy dogs and allowed inmates with mental-health issues to stroke them and play fetch the ball. The contact with these animals led to big behaviour changes, including increased calmness in the inmates; as one reported: 'I don't know what it is, but even when I am running around with him [the therapy dog] I just feel better inside, calmer, more peaceful.' These calming effects were often long lasting; as another inmate put it: 'I just walk around for the rest of the day on cloud nine.' After spending time with these furry friends, some participants in the trial were also able to regulate their emotions better, talking about things they struggled to address before.[191]

Prisons are just the start, and animals are being used in many other venues to help give people a mental-health boost, from psychiatric hospitals to soothing the nerves of anxious flyers in airports. Emotional-support animals, which are thought to be able to help people with mental-health conditions including depression and PTSD, comprise not just cats and dogs but a menagerie including rabbits, hamsters, ducks, peacocks and more. Pets aren't simply a poor substitute for human company; they have their unique qualities, too. As one of the inmates in the prison trial pointed out, dogs don't judge you on your past transgressions. And you can't take it personally if a cat is being standoffish – it's just their way.

Not everyone is convinced that this obsession with the soothing effects of animals is a good one, however. Partly that's because of the mixed results in the research. Until we have more conclusive evidence, some of these claims remain on shaky ground. You might argue that this doesn't matter as long as people feel better for it. Recent surveys of both cat and dog owners show many of them believe their pets have been instrumental in maintaining their mental health, especially cats.[192]

Professionals are of the same view. One survey found that 97 per cent of doctors believed in the health benefits of having a pet.[193] But some experts are worried that people encouraged to take on a pet for health reasons might underestimate the work involved, to the detriment of the animal.[194]

Of course, there can be downsides to owning a pet, too. The death of an animal may be hard to handle, especially if your pet is a strong tie to someone you have lost already. And research shows that some people avoid seeking help for serious medical problems for fear of losing their pet when they do.

Mixed evidence

Where does this leave us? If you have a pet already, or are seriously thinking of getting one, the likelihood is you're already sold on the benefits. For those looking to animals for a health fix in response to specific issues, the evidence should be handled with caution and it is likely animals will benefit some groups more than others. A 2020 review of the evidence found that in older people, at least, companion animals can help reduce symptoms of mental-health issues including depression, anxiety, cognitive

---

FIVE WAYS PETS CAN HELP WITH DEMENTIA

Animal-assisted therapy, in which an animal becomes part of the treatment process, has been tested in a number of studies for people with dementia and has been found to have numerous benefits. These include increased physical activity, less loneliness, and short-term improvements in memory and communication skills. People in nursing homes with dementia given weekly access to animal-assisted therapy saw benefits to their levels of agitation and aggression. And the introduction of aquaria into specialist units for people with Alzheimer's disease has even been shown to improve their nutrition after two weeks. The advantage of this over getting a pet is that it doesn't involve ownership, which can be too much of a commitment. However, one recent study did find that ownership was important, showing that those people with dementia who had a pet were more likely to walk for three hours a week and to feel less lonely, but only if they were involved in caring for the animal. Those who had a pet but weren't the ones who cared for it had increased depression and a worse quality of life than those who had no pet at all.

impairment and the behavioural and psychiatric symptoms of dementia.[195] But when it came to physical health, the findings were a lot less convincing. If doctors are going to be prescribing pets to people, the evidence needs to be up to scratch.

In the meantime, there are other options. The Japanese craze for pet cafes is spreading, so finding somewhere to sip a tea while stroking a cat or a rabbit might provide a quick fix. There's certainly evidence that people find animals calming and that stroking them can lower blood pressure and boost feel-good brain chemicals.

Researchers are also busy looking into whether robotic pets might be able to provide the health benefits without the need to poop and scoop. Besides, pets are only one part of the solution. An Australian study from 2021 has also shown that when people encountered animals in the wild, it led to feelings of love, belonging, positivity and a gain of perspective. What's more, it also enhanced reciprocity, meaning they were more likely to give back and care for the wildlife and animals around them too[196] – a win-win for animal lovers and animals alike.

CHAPTER 23

The mood-boosting benefits of light and dark

On the next cloudless night, take a look at the sky. Can you see the Milky Way? If so, lucky you. Two-thirds of Europeans and 80 per cent of North Americans can't catch a glimpse of it as a result of light pollution. It's a problem that afflicts 80 per cent of the globe, and is on the rise – earth's artificially lit outdoor area is estimated to be growing at about 2 per cent each year.

That matters, because artificial lighting is messing with our bodies. Animals on earth, humans included, evolved to a twenty-four-hour cycle of night and day. Before the advent of artificial lighting, our ancestors would have spent the night either asleep or gathered round the warm glow of a campfire if not finding their way with a candle or oil lamp. They would have woken up to natural daylight, and spent many hours outdoors.

Today, not only do we spend the majority of our time indoors (some estimates suggest that for Westerners it is 90 per cent of their time, and that was before the pandemic saw the amount of indoor time across much of the world increase by on average 35 per cent), but artificial lighting accompanies us well past dusk, and even floods our rooms when we are sleeping.

Light nights …

The fact that we rarely experience darkness at night is one of three crucial ways that our modern-day relationship with light is having an adverse impact on our mental health.

Understanding why starts with a surprisingly recent discovery that revolutionized our understanding of the way humans detect light. You've probably heard about the rods and cones that line the retina at the back of your eye (see the diagram below). Cones are useful for colour vision, while the rods detect light and are helpful for seeing in more obscure lighting. But astonishingly, it wasn't until 1999 that Russell Foster at the University of Oxford and his colleagues discovered a whole new set of sensors, behind the rods and cones, whose job it is to measure light and synchronize our body clocks to our environment. Incidentally, this is how people who are blind can still maintain their circadian rhythm even though their rods and cones aren't working (and is why, if they have their eyes removed, they experience a profound shifting of their body clocks).

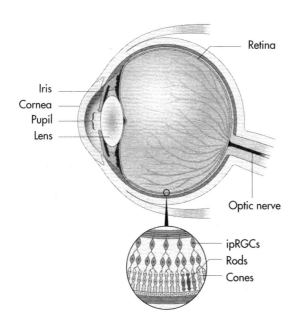

Retina

Iris
Cornea
Pupil
Lens

Optic nerve

ipRGCs
Rods
Cones

This third kind of receptor, helpfully named the 'intrinsically photosensitive retinal ganglion cells', or ipRGCs for short, fire in response to any type of bright light, but are particularly sensitive to blue light. This is the kind of light we would normally experience in the earlier hours of the day, because sunlight contains more blue light in the morning, turning to a redder light at dusk. When light hits the eye's ipRGCs cells, they send signals that directly act on the master clock in the brain, a small patch of cells called the suprachiasmatic nucleus (SCN), telling it what time of the day or night it is. The SCN in turn controls the ticking of body clocks in the cells throughout our body, keeping all our organs and systems working in sync. And this master clock also sets the timer for the release of melatonin, a hormone that increases at night telling us it's time to go to sleep.

This newly discovered set of cells is therefore vital for setting our body clock, instructing our brain about when we should be up and when it's time for bed, and making sure the entire body works as a coordinated whole.

But there is more. These cells also talk directly to areas of the brain involved in controlling our emotions, and so the concern is that interfering with their signalling could play a role in mood disorders. Animal studies lend weight to the idea, as messing with lighting in mice's cages can lead to depression-like symptoms, and there is now a growing medical consensus that exposure to light at the wrong time – in other words, at night – could be affecting our mood.

One way this extraneous light might be playing havoc with our emotions is simply through sleep. Even low levels of light at night can strongly inhibit melatonin production, which can force our body clocks into a later cycle, causing us to become more owlish – and you don't need to be glued to your phone to be affected. Light intensity is commonly measured in lux, and the illumination of a residential side street is about 5 lux. By comparison, an overcast night sky would measure just 0.00003 to 0.0001 lux, and a full moon normally registers between 0.1 to 0.3 lux. In 2016, the American Medical Association issued a report against using blue-rich LED streetlights, because of their detrimental effect on our health, but even standard lighting can affect our sleep, with studies showing that indoor lights, such as e-readers and night-lights, can interfere with sleep duration and sleep quality. People who sleep with a night-light of 40 lux, for instance, have been found to have shallower sleep and more arousals in the night. And outdoor light pollution has been associated in large studies with poor sleep, daytime sleepiness, increased snoring and insomnia, all of which can have a devastating effect on mood and mental health.

Sleep is not the whole story, however, because mice exposed to light at the wrong time can get symptoms of depression without any change to their sleep. Hormones are probably playing a role here. Take glucocorticoids, which are involved in regulating our stress response and implicated in some patients with major depression; these rely on bright light first thing in the morning to function properly.

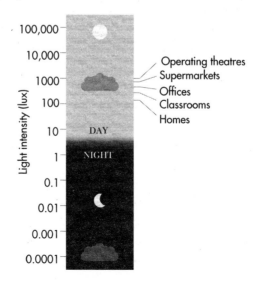

THE COGNITIVE EFFECTS OF LIGHT

Exposure to the wrong light at the wrong time is bad for our moods, but what about cognition? Jet lag is a helpful proxy here, as mice subjected to jet lag have memory problems and decreased neurogenesis in the hippocampus. Flight attendants also suffer: long-haul flights with short recovery times have been shown to lead to a 10 per cent decrease in reaction times and other cognitive deficits, as well as a shrinking of certain brain areas. Very recent research also suggests that better light in the daytime could improve learning and memory in college students. Because of the effect of lighting on the brain, including sleep, circadian rhythm and cognition, some researchers have come to the view that simply changing the lightbulbs could be an incredibly simple way to improve the educational attainment of all children. Our cognitive abilities might also vary over the year, according to one study that showed that when faced with cognitive tasks, the brain activity in areas involved in memory and attention had seasonal peaks. One idea is that the brain has to work harder in various ways to compensate for the effects of the seasons in order to maintain a constant level of performance. If that's true, it could be that this system isn't working properly in people with seasonal affective disorder, who tend to feel blue during winter.

Worryingly, exposure to light at night could also cause changes to the structure and function of the brain. Mice exposed to continuous light had less neurogenesis in their hippocampi, which coincided with depression-like behaviour. The effect wasn't as bad with red light as with blue – exactly the kind of light given off by our screens and bright artificial lighting. Exposure to the wrong light at the wrong time could also affect our gene activity – including those genes involved in psychiatric disorders – not least because 20 per cent of all our genes are expressed according to our circadian rhythms.[197] And this light is also likely to affect the way the signalling chemicals in our brains called neurotransmitters operate.

Taken together, the evidence strongly points to the idea that getting too much light at night is not a bright idea. The problem is that because most of us are exposed to light pollution, it's hard to gauge just how bad it is. Two insights from very different populations can help to shed clarity on the situation.

One of these involves people living in Finland, north of the Arctic Circle, where the sun does not set for sixty successive days in the summer, during which time there are reports of dramatic increases in violent suicides.[198] The other concerns Old Order Amish, who live a pre-industrialization lifestyle, and avoid artificial lighting. A 2020 study in which a group of Amish wore activity- and light-tracking devices showed just how different their relationship with sunlight is.[199] The Amish were revealed to be very active first thing in the morning and then reduced their activity towards bedtime, going to bed at sunset. Unlike the Finns, the Amish also have very strong patterns of light and dark. During the day, light exposure was in excess of 1,000 lux (by comparison, our homes and offices tend to be lit to around 100 to 300 lux), and in the evening they were exposed to less than 10 lux, dropping to just 1 lux when they were sleeping. Notably, the Amish have remarkably low rates of depression.

... and dark days

If these populations teach us anything it's that too much light at night is a bad idea. The Amish in this study also hint at another way our relationship with light is off kilter. As well as being exposed to brighter lights at night, our daylight hours are spent in relative gloom, causing a flattening of our circadian rhythms.

Your home or office may feel bright, but in reality it's closer to dusk than to daytime. Most indoor lighting comes in at around

100 to 300 lux, whereas even an overcast day is around 1,000, rising to more than 100,000 lux in direct sunlight.

Early-morning exposure to bright light is especially important for setting our circadian clock, which might be one reason for all the low mood and sleep disturbances that have been reported during the pandemic, with so many people working from home.

One well-cited study shows just how strong this effect is: it found that people who were exposed to bright light between the hours of eight in the morning and twelve noon took on average eighteen minutes to fall asleep at night, compared to forty-five minutes for those exposed to low light levels. They also slept for twenty minutes longer,[200] and other studies show that exposure to bright light in the day leads to less disrupted and fragmented sleep at night.

That blue morning light also makes us feel more alert, even in low doses, with an hour of exposure to low intensity blue light resulting in levels of alertness equivalent to drinking a double espresso.[201]

With this in mind, there are simple things you can do to boost your exposure to this all-important light (see the box opposite), including getting out first thing in the morning.

Another useful but underappreciated advantage to getting a hit of light early on in the day is that it could buffer against the effects of exposure to blue light at the wrong time. One study found that three hours was the required amount, and the bright light early in the day also improved participants' reaction speeds – with this cognitive boost lasting well into the day. In other words, not only does bright light enhance your mood and your alertness; the strong effect on your body clock could also counterbalance the detrimental effect of being exposed to it later at night – a handy life hack for anyone who likes to indulge in evening screen time.[202]

HOW TO HACK YOUR LIGHT EXPOSURE FOR BETTER BRAIN HEALTH

- Build outdoor time into your day. Choose sitting outside for breakfast or lunch, exercise outside, and consider walking or cycling for part of your commute if possible.
- While you're at it, grab a coffee – blue light and caffeine is a combination that, taken together, can improve mood.
- Moving just a few feet from the window causes a significant drop in lux, so wherever you can when indoors, pick the window seat.
- Rather than fight the winter darkness using artificial lighting, why not embrace the long evenings and adopt a hygge style of cosy comfort, with low lighting or candles.
- If you have children, swap their night-light for one that emits red rather than blue light for a better quality of sleep.

Feeling blue

That brings us to the third way that light affects our mental health – our love affair with our screens. Because of the blue light they emit these devices have become public enemy number one when it comes to circadian health and good sleep.

How seriously should we take the claims? Let's remember that the ipRGCs in the eye are more readily activated by blue light. One frequently cited study found that people take longer to fall asleep if they read an e-reader before bed rather than a normal book.[203] Aside from shifting melatonin production, and therefore our body clock, light from phones and tablets affects slow-wave sleep, which we know is the deep restorative kind. It also impacts on growth hormones, so children who look at screens before bed could see a change in their growth and brain development. Teenagers living in urban environments with more outside lighting are more likely to be night owls, and the same goes for those using electronic media in the evening. Even the glymphatic system, that all-important brain-cleaning network that kicks in at night, may be subject to circadian rhythms, so by shifting our body clocks we might be impacting on the brain's vital self-cleaning abilities.

All this makes a strong case for banning phones from the bedroom, but some argue that the issue is overblown. One recent study looking at screen-use found that to disrupt melatonin production you'd need to be exposed to 85 lux for an hour – which is about what you'd get from an tablet, but not from a phone. There's another reason your phone might keep you awake at night though. Whether you're scrolling on social media, checking tomorrow's to-do list or planning your next holiday, the content can be overly stimulating, getting your brain whirring just when you want to be winding down. So if you can bear it, you'd do well to leave your phone outside the bedroom, or at the very least switch it off an hour before bed, keeping that ultra-blue light for the morning when we need it most.

Some people, however, including shift workers, have no choice but to stay alert when their body and mind should be switching off. Our circadian rhythms become blunted as we age, and less light also gets through to the retina, meaning that older people, too, are already at more of a risk of circadian disruption. Then there are particular groups, such as those in hospital and in care homes, who are often subjected to bright levels of light during the night – either for their safety or simply because they are on a busy ward.

One very recent study has found that giving people in care homes more blue-enriched light during the day, and less at night, results in fewer falls. And if you give better lighting to nurses in ICU, medical errors go down by a third. These kinds of impacts could lead to billions in health savings, and potentially lives saved too, all by something as simple as changing the lighting.

CHAPTER 24

Nature is good for mental health

Next time you need a pick-me-up try having a long soak … in nature. The Japanese practice of *shinrin yoku* or 'forest-bathing' is a well-established tradition of encouraging people to spend time outdoors, connecting with nature through all the senses. It became popular after studies showed the calming effects on both body and mind, reducing heart rate, stress hormones and blood pressure.

We've known for a long time that spending time outdoors is good for physical health, but in the last decade an explosion of research has found just how good it is for our mental wellbeing too. One of the first striking findings came in 2013 when Dr Mathew White, at the University of Exeter in the UK, and his colleagues followed people who had moved house and found significant benefits to mental wellbeing when they moved to greener urban areas.[204]

Natural connection

Just at a time when more of us are living in urban environments than ever before (according to the UN, two-thirds of us will be living in cities in 2050),[205] we have discovered that the benefits of spending time outdoors extend way beyond the stress-busting effects of forest-bathing. Connecting with nature has been found to improve mood, happiness and wellbeing as well as decreasing mental distress.[206] Our thinking skills can benefit too, with time in nature shown to improve attention and memory, creativity, imagination, and children's academic performance. It improves social interaction, and can give people a greater sense of meaning to their lives. It can also improve sleep and has been shown to help people with conditions including depression, anxiety and attention deficit hyperactivity disorder (ADHD). Some doctors have even begun prescribing time in nature for their patients.

That nature can be such a tonic will come as little surprise to many an outdoorsy type. And that makes sense – our species didn't evolve to live in the city. Biologist E. O. Wilson explains this in terms of the biophilia hypothesis, which says that our brains are wired to seek out a connection to nature because of the environment we evolved in – which is very different to that we live in today. In other words, our early environment shaped our brain.

Another popular explanation is known as attention restoration theory. In a nutshell, this is the idea that our ability to concentrate is restored by time spent in nature. Attention can be divided into two types: involuntary, in which our attention is captured by intriguing or important stimuli (an intimate conversation between a couple sitting at a table behind you in a cafe, for instance), and directed or voluntary attention, where you actively focus on something (the book you were trying to read before you started eavesdropping). This requires what psychologists call 'top-down' control, which means that our thoughts are controlling our actions. In contrast, 'bottom-up' thinking is where sensory information is influencing our thoughts. During directed attention, we also need to suppress distractions, which is mentally exhausting.

This is where nature comes in. It is bursting with subtle, inherently fascinating and eye-catching stimuli, which easily trigger the bottom-up, involuntary kind of attention that gives the thinking mind a break, therefore enabling attention to replenish. If you've ever felt revived after watching a glorious sunset or

TIPS FOR MAKING THE MOST OF NATURE

- Wear a watch: the health benefits of time in nature kick in after about two hours a week, according to a study of almost twenty thousand people. Any more than that was better still, up until five hours. After this point, the benefits plateau.

- Do it your way: it doesn't matter whether that time is spent all in one go or broken up into lots of little chunks during the week. One study found that the shortest time to have an effect was ten minutes – so make that the minimum.

- Make a connection: the advantages of being outdoors are particularly strong if you feel connected to nature, so find ways to engage with it, whether that's watching the changing seasons, gardening, or spotting birds, trees and other wildlife.

- Wrap up warm: the mental-health benefits apply not just in the summer but in winter too, when many of us need it most, so try to keep that connection going all year round.

- Do it on your terms: people with mental-health conditions such as depression and anxiety feel better when they spend time in nature, but it has to be their choice (so nature 'prescriptions' that are being given in several countries could backfire). When they felt social pressure to do it, they felt less happiness and more anxiety about the outing.

- Quality over quantity: the specific qualities of green space seem to be more important than how big the space is. Two qualities in particular have been shown to reduce stress: spaces that act as a refuge, and those that really feel like you are in nature. Refuge tends to be defined as those spaces surrounded by bushes and vegetation where people feel safe. Spending time in places that feel particularly serene is also linked to a decreased risk of mental illness in women.

gazing at the trees swaying in the breeze, it might be because these sights have given a break to the top-down processes you need for work, concentration and focus.

Urban environments are thought to be less restorative because they are not so passive, instead grabbing our attention suddenly and requiring action. If we're jumping out of the way of fast-moving traffic there is no chance for the brain to get that much-needed respite.[207]

There might be additional reasons your brain will benefit from time spent in nature. More time in daylight is an obvious advantage, which as we know can improve our mood, tune our circadian rhythms and improve sleep. And lower levels of air or noise pollution can both have a positive impact on mental health.

The way we relate to our green spaces also has a special role to play. White has done research measuring the amount of nature people have around their homes, as well as other factors such as how much time they spend there and what they are doing during this time. His team also collected data on measures like how people rated their wellbeing, as well as on medical prescriptions for anxiety and depression. He was surprised to find that the biggest predictor of positive mental health was not proximity or time spent in nature, but people's psychological connectedness to it.[208] Of course, the best scenario is that you live near to it, spend lots of time in it, and also feel that connection.

There's more reason than ever, then, to head out to your local park or green space and, if you are already thinking of the many positive mental-health benefits of exercise, you might opt to build up a sweat outside, rather than in the gym, to get twice the hit.

Positive waves

If you are lucky enough to live by a sea, ocean or lake, the benefits should be even greater. In the last few years, several studies including a large consortium of European researchers have turned their attention to these 'blue spaces'. When blue spaces are pitted against green spaces such as forests and parks, the blue ones consistently score better, and the best of all is living somewhere where they meet.

White points out that when it comes to wellbeing, the effects of nature are only going to be marginal compared to 'big ticket' factors such as employment, marital satisfaction and that your children are happy. That said, his research has found that living near blue spaces can buffer against some of the mental-health inequalities driven by socioeconomic differences. Whereas woodlands tend to be used predominantly by the middle classes, the beach is used by everyone across society. And two large studies have now shown that poorer people who live by the sea are healthier both mentally and physically than they should be given those big-ticket drivers of wellbeing such as unemployment and deprivation. They are still less healthy than their wealthier counterparts, but not as much as you would expect, so living near the coast closes the gap on health inequality.

Why is it that blue spaces do better than green? Several themes emerge from studies that have asked people about their experience. One is that blue spaces, especially the coast, often involve patterns of change that you don't get with green spaces. The tide ebbs and flows, the waves repeatedly lap at the shore. As well as this movement there are changes in sound and even light that you don't experience in the park or a forest, and these constant changes capture the attention in a way that fits with attention restoration theory. There's an unthreatening energy to these captivating environmental shifts and they trigger what scientists call 'soft fascination', diverting our attention from more specific thoughts – possibly even the negative ruminative thoughts that are associated with depression.

The other thing the studies have found is that blue spaces afford certain kinds of behaviours that green spaces do not – playing in the sand, swimming, paddling and so on. Children say that their parents play and engage with them more when they go to the sea. These kinds of activities seem to be building strong positive social experiences with friends and family, and this quality-time in turn is more beneficial for mood and wellbeing.

THE BENEFITS FOR KIDS

Every parent of small children will have experienced the desperate urge to just get out of the house, and the apparently magical restorative benefits of even a short trip to the local park. There's probably more going on there than just letting out some pent-up energy. The benefits of getting into nature for kids are huge, ranging from better academic performance to improved mood and focus, and helping with ADHD. Childhood experience of nature can also boost environmentalism in adulthood. And having access to urban green spaces can also play a role in children's social networks and friendships, even promoting social inclusion across cultures.

The seaside likewise works wonders. Dr Mathew White has done research with children who had been expelled from school or were at risk of expulsion because of behavioural issues, and were enrolled in a twelve-week surfing programme. As well as becoming fitter, the kids ended up with more positive attitudes towards their schools and their friendships, and also had a more positive body image, which is especially important because in the early teenage years it's one of the biggest predictors of overall wellbeing.

Next best thing

If you really can't make it out into nature, there are ways to reap the same benefits from the comfort of your own home. Studies have found that simply looking at pictures of nature or watching natural-history documentaries can mimic some of the effects, increasing positivity and beating boredom. Connectedness again seems to be key here. In one recent experiment comparing how people responded to watching footage from a natural-history film either on standard television, in a 360 degrees experience, or in full virtual reality, the biggest improvements to mood came from watching it in VR because viewers could interact with the physical space around them.

As virtual-reality technology becomes more sophisticated and more affordable, there is huge potential to recreate the mood-boosting influence of nature for people with mobility issues. This virtual natural environment could also help those who are struggling to leave their home because of depression, potentially improving their symptoms enough that they could eventually want to venture out.

VR has promise in clinical settings too. One study found that people who took a virtual-reality stroll by the beach while they were having a tooth extraction experienced less pain, anxiety and stress, and also felt much happier about returning to the dentist later on than those who took a virtual walk round a town, or had no virtual-reality aspect at all. Researchers are now looking into whether other elements of nature, such as sounds and smells, might be incorporated. One day it might even be possible to develop specially tailored virtual-reality trips to nature that give a memory boost to people with dementia and other forms of memory loss.

Finally, all this could be good news for nature, too. When people live closer to nature and spend more time connecting with it, they also develop more pro-environment behaviour, such as recycling and volunteering for environmental causes.[209]

PART 6

HEALTHY BODY, HEALTHY MIND

It's understandable that many adults dread the creep towards middle age. Our bodies are designed to reach peak performance in time for our reproductive years. Once our genes have, in theory at least, been passed on to future generations, we start to fray around the edges. Little glitches mean more damage to DNA, a less efficient immune system, a foggier head … the list goes on. But even if ageing is inevitable, the amount by which our bodies age, and how fast, is in large part within our control.

One of the most important examples of this is the immune system. Inflammation, the body's first-line response to injury or infection, keeps us healthy when we are in trouble, but too much inflammation, for too long, can have a disastrous effect on both the body and mind. Inflammation ticks up as we age, but if we look at those people who have reached the ripe old age of one hundred, their levels of inflammation look like those of someone forty years younger. This 'biological' as opposed to chronological age is largely a reflection of lifestyle choices.

Aside from the brain, the immune system is probably the most complex system in your body, and we are only just starting to get to grips with the way it connects to the health of the mind. Even so, there is plenty to be getting on with if we want some of what those centenarians are having, and would like to keep our immune system younger than our years and our inflammation in check. And the best place to start is the right diet and exercise.

There are other, much more simple ways to protect our brain as we age too, and we explore two of these in this section. One is dental hygiene. What do your teeth have to do with your brain? Possibly a lot, if a new theory of Alzheimer's is to be believed. And while you're at it, take care of your hearing. Because of the stigma around hearing aids and the implicit notion that you are getting old if you need to wear one, many people with hearing problems go decades without seeking proper treatment. Yet hearing loss is one of the largest preventable risk factors for dementia, and getting help for it can contribute to undoing some of the harm. Which all goes to show how taking care of our physical health can have life-changing effects on cognition and mental wellbeing, too.

CHAPTER 25

Inflammation can mess with your mind

Our immune system evolved to protect us. Then modern life came along. The way many of us live today is causing the immune system to run amok, and it has now been implicated in many diseases of the body and mind, from asthma and arthritis to depression and Alzheimer's disease. The culprit is inflammation, the body's first line of defence against invasion from foreign bodies such as bacteria and viruses.

Inflammation is a blunt tool that responds to any kind of infection or injury. Imagine you cut your hand with a dirty knife. The job of the inflammatory response is to quickly send immune cells to the scene to kill any pathogens, such as bacteria, that have entered the body, and then set the stage for repair to the wound. First, blood rushes to the infected area, causing heat and redness as blood vessels dilate. This increased blood flow carries with it important molecules, including immune cells such as white blood cells. The blood vessels also become more leaky, allowing immune molecules to flood the infected area, which causes swelling. Specialized immune cells delivered to the site are now able to destroy and gobble up any bacteria from the knife like a microscopic Pac-Man, and clean up the mess so that tissue repair can begin.

So far, so useful. But problems arise when the way we live today throws this carefully evolved system out of kilter. Stress is one of the big culprits (as we discuss in more detail in Chapter 29) because, in our evolutionary past, feeling stressed was a sign that we were at risk of encountering some kind of attack and potential injury – a tiger bite rather than that kitchen knife – and therefore primes the immune system to be ready for infection. Prolonged stress keeps the immune system, and inflammation, switched on too long.

Obesity is another contributor, because fat cells store large quantities of inflammatory molecules called cytokines. These can leak out when we accumulate large fat stores, causing constant low-level inflammation. Putting on too much weight can also upset the gut microbiome, causing the gut to become leaky, which also triggers inflammation.[210]

Immune age

Some factors are harder to control. As we age, it's normal for levels of inflammation to creep up, a process known as 'inflammaging'. Because inflammation has now been implicated in so many diseases, especially those to which we are more prone with age, there is growing interest from scientists as to how we might use the immune system – in particular, inflammation – as a measure of people's 'biological age'.

The idea of biological age is that if you had two people with the same number of candles on their birthday cake, one of them might be a lot younger physically because of their lifestyle, and therefore would be likely to live longer – this person would have a lower biological age, even if their chronological age is the same. There are different approaches to measuring someone's biological age, but the level of inflammation is particularly appealing because we already have drugs available that treat inflammation. And because lifestyle factors also play into it, there are lots of possible ways we might reverse the inflammation clock.

Why does inflammation increase as we get older? One cause

is that some immune cells start to behave erratically as we age, including neutrophils, one of the types of cells that flood out of blood vessels during inflammation in order to destroy any harmful invading pathogens. In our later decades, these cells lose their sense of direction, becoming worse at detecting foreign bodies, clumsily crashing about causing carnage as they work, triggering even more inflammation. Fortunately, there are some simple ways to keep this process in check – taking statins and getting in ten thousand steps a day have both been shown to keep our neutrophils young.

For now there are no widely available tests of your inflammation age, but scientists are working on it. In 2021, researchers in the US developed the first inflammation ageing clock, called iAge, which measures people's levels of chronic inflammation and predicts their risk of age-related disorders such as neurodegenerative diseases. The tool was developed using the chronological age and measures of health from over a thousand people ranging from eight to ninety-six years old.[211] When the team tested the clock on a group of centenarians, they found that their iAge age was on average forty years younger than their chronological age, showing how important inflammation is for healthy ageing. The hope is that being able to measure inflammation easily, for instance with a blood test, would give us a way to keep a watchful eye on our biological age, and take steps to prevent further damage with drugs and lifestyle changes when needed, possibly even reversing the clock.

Sickness behaviour

Another reason why it will be so useful to be able to measure people's baseline levels of chronic inflammation is the effect it has on the brain. As well as sending an army of cells to the site of the wound or trauma to destroy any invading pathogens, inflammation also sends messengers to the brain, which houses its own immune system, separated from the body by the blood–brain barrier. Here, the brain's system of neuro-inflammation kicks in, triggering the kinds of behaviours we experience when we are sick – lethargy, a loss of appetite, social withdrawal, sleepiness and depressed mood: very similar behaviours to those we see in depression.

This is extremely useful when we are actually poorly – staying at home tucked under a duvet means we will rest, allowing the body to divert its energy away from other tasks and concentrate on doing what it needs to do to make us better. It also means we are less likely to go about spreading a possible infection to others.

But if inflammation remains high because of our lifestyle, it can signal the brain to keep up these sickness behaviours when it doesn't need them, and there is now plenty of evidence linking depression and the immune system. People with diseases that are known to overly activate the immune system have higher rates of depression, including those with type 2 diabetes, who have twice the rate of depression as the general population.[212] More than a third of people with asthma, which is caused by inflammation in the lungs, have depression, and those with both asthma and depression tend to experience especially high levels of one type of inflammatory cytokine.[213] Children who have high measures of inflammation are also more likely to suffer from bouts of depression when they reach the age of eighteen.

The obvious question, then, is whether drugs that help to dampen down inflammation might also alleviate some of the symptoms of depression. After all, we have an arsenal of anti-inflammatory drugs already approved and used every day by millions of people at our disposal, including bog-standard aspirin, statins and some antibiotics. Some of the evidence on this front is looking promising. A recent study that pooled together results from twenty-six different studies testing various anti-inflammatory drugs found that they were 52 per cent better at reducing symptoms of depression overall, and 79 per cent better at eliminating symptoms, compared to a placebo. They were even more effective when used in conjunction with standard antidepressant treatments.[214]

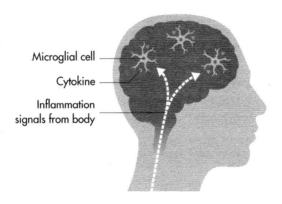

Microglial cell

Cytokine

Inflammation signals from body

Off switch

Most of the anti-inflammatory drugs that we have work by stopping inflammation from happening in the first place, but there might also be another option: a potential 'off switch' for inflammation. A recent discovery that the immune system produces chemicals called resolvins, whose job it is to switch off inflammation when the source of harm has been taken care of, and the finding that these don't seem to be produced properly in people with chronic inflammation, offers up another possible treatment route. Current anti-inflammatory drugs that prevent the immune response from kicking in can leave people at risk of infection, so a treatment that switches the system off when needed would be preferable. And research is now underway into drugs that might do this.

But anti-inflammatories – whether they stop inflammation from switching on, or help to turn it off – won't be a silver bullet for depression. About a third of people with depression have high levels of inflammation, so this appears to be just one

WHAT CAN YOU DO TO REDUCE INFLAMMATION?

- Resolvins, the chemicals that the body produces to switch off inflammation, are made from omega-3 fatty acids. So make sure you're getting plenty of these, and the best source is oily fish like salmon.
- A healthy diet can help to protect against inflammation. Opt for fresh fruit and vegetables, as well as whole grains, and avoid too much sugar and processed foods that contain sweeteners and emulsifiers.
- Regularly practising yoga has been found to reduce inflammation, possibly by decreasing stress levels. And studies in rats suggest that stretching might also directly soothe inflamed muscles.
- Exercise that builds up muscle such as walking, running or resistance training is another strategy. Skeletal muscle regulates inflammation, and people who get in ten thousand steps a day have younger-looking immune cells.
- Losing excess body fat will reduce the number of inflammatory cytokines that leak out of fat, and so help to reduce chronic inflammation.

underlying cause of a complex and multifaceted condition. It certainly won't work for everyone. And in some people, such a treatment could even be harmful. Several studies have found that anti-inflammatories only helped those people with depression who have high levels of inflammation to start with.[215] In others, it actually made their symptoms worse. So getting the right drug to the right patients will be key.

It will also be important to work out why, when so many of us walk around with chronic levels of inflammation due to stress, obesity, ageing and other lifestyle factors, only some people get depression. One answer might be that there is a threshold level of inflammation that tips people over the edge. That means individuals who are predisposed to high levels of inflammation, potentially because of early childhood trauma, might be at increased risk – another reason why an inflammation clock will be a particularly useful tool.

Inflammation has also been implicated in Alzheimer's disease, although exactly the role it plays is far from clear. People with Alzheimer's tend to have higher levels of inflammatory cytokines in the brain, but it isn't entirely obvious whether they are a consequence of the amyloid deposits that form during the disease, or whether they might be a cause.

One theory is that immune cells in the brain called microglia struggle to clear the Alzheimer's plaques, causing microglia to remain constantly activated. Then, when inflammation strikes because of other lifestyle factors such as obesity, the ensuing signals to the brain send these immune cells into overdrive, and they end up killing brain cells.

However, in 2020, researchers in the US found that one inflammatory protein, produced in response to infections, directly causes plaques to be laid down in the brain, and that removing it in the brain of mice decreased the amount of amyloid present, suggesting that inflammation itself could be causing amyloid to build up. As with depression, the hope is that making sense of the role of inflammation in Alzheimer's will lead to new treatments, although drug trials for Alzheimer's are even harder to carry out, not least because of the slow progression of the disease meaning that trials are slow and very expensive.

Still, what is abundantly clear is that in the wrong situations, our immune system is not always acting in our best interests. It isn't visible like many other signs of health, but its vital role in our physical and mental wellbeing means we need to look after it. And thankfully, there are plenty of things we can do to keep it fighting for us, rather than against us.

To help avoid Alzheimer's, take care of your teeth

If a fear of the dentist chair keeps you from regular check-ups or seeking help for bleeding gums, here is some news that might well change your mind. In 2019, a radical new idea emerged that challenged our understanding of what causes Alzheimer's, and other diseases too. And it all starts with your teeth.

As we saw in earlier chapters, the prevailing view is that Alzheimer's disease is caused by the accumulation of toxic plaques of a protein called beta-amyloid – the amyloid hypothesis – as well as tangles of a protein called tau within nerve cells themselves. These proteins kill off brain cells, or stop them communicating effectively, which is thought to cause the symptoms of the disease. And yet, after decades of research, this explanation has fallen flat for two crucial reasons. One is that many people who have these signs of Alzheimer's in the brain do not develop the symptoms of dementia, whereas other people who have dementia remain largely free of these plaques and tangles.

Even more damning is that decades of clinical trials for treatments that either block amyloid from forming, or remove the plaques, have shown little success in actually reducing the cognitive decline that comes with the disease. In 2021, much hype was made when the drug aducanumab, a vaccine with antibodies against beta-amyloid, was approved by the FDA – the first Alzheimer's drug in eighteen years to get this seal of approval. Unfortunately, the decision was controversial, in large part because trial results focused on the ability of the drug to clear the plaques, but hadn't shown it to be overly effective in reducing the symptoms of the disease, and also because some people experienced strong side effects.[216] So much money has been spent on developing drugs to tackle amyloid plaques and, with so little progress, many believe we might be barking up the wrong tree.

Root cause

Our mouths are host to thousands of species of bacteria, with harmful ones kept in check by good bacteria that promote healthy teeth and gums. Bacteria form a thin film on the teeth called plaque, and if this is allowed to build up and harden it can pierce the gum and trigger inflammation. This is an appropriate immune response to invading microbes, designed to kill off the invaders, but if it goes on for too long it can build up pockets of infection under the gum. *Porphyromonas gingivalis*, the key bacterium implicated in gum disease, thrives in this environment. What's more, it has some crafty tricks to wreak havoc on the immune system.

First, it is able to block some parts of the inflammatory response while keeping others active, which generates long-lasting but very ineffective inflammation. This weakened immune response doesn't manage to kill off the bacteria, but eventually starts to destroy our own cells.

Once the gum is infected, *P. gingivalis* can also make its way into our cells, including white blood cells, a key part of the immune system itself. Coursing through our bodies by hitching a ride within these cells, the bacterium is able to evade our immune response and invade distant organs far from the site of infection in our mouths. Eventually, *P. gingivalis* can reach and enter the brain, most likely using this Trojan horse approach to penetrate the blood–brain barrier, which is supposed to keep microbes from invading the brain.

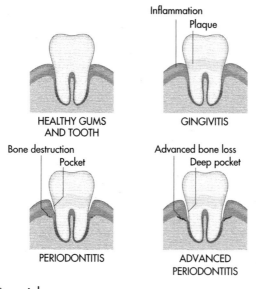

Inflammation
Plaque

**HEALTHY GUMS
AND TOOTH**

GINGIVITIS

Bone destruction
Pocket

Advanced bone loss
Deep pocket

PERIODONTITIS

**ADVANCED
PERIODONTITIS**

DNA evidence

As *P. gingivalis* is so good at hiding in plain sight, its possible role in Alzheimer's was missed for a long time. But technology that detects fragments of bacterial DNA has shed new light on the idea, and in the last few years a convergence of evidence builds a pretty compelling picture. In 2019, a team of researchers including some from the biotech company Cortexyme conducted post-mortems on the brains of people with Alzheimer's and found that the majority contained two toxic digestive enzymes that *P. gingivalis* uses to break down human proteins, in the hippocampus, which we know is implicated in the memory loss associated with Alzheimer's. The more of these toxins – called gingipains – there were, the greater the amount of tau too. They also found DNA from the bacterium in the cerebral cortex, which is important for information and language processing, and conceptual thought, as well as in the cerebrospinal fluid of living Alzheimer's patients.

HOW TO AVOID GUM DISEASE

Gum disease is extremely common. While estimates vary by country, age group and severity of the disease, it affects around half of adults. In its earlier and milder stages it is known as gingivitis, which if left untreated develops to the more serious form, periodontitis. Gum disease is caused by an accumulation of bacteria on the teeth and gums in a film called plaque. Symptoms include receding gums and bleeding. If plaque builds up and hardens it can penetrate the gum causing inflammation and help bacteria get into the bloodstream. Eventually, the tooth may have to be removed. As gum disease has been linked to Alzheimer's disease, it's more important than ever to take oral hygiene seriously. Here's what you can do:

- Sore gums, bleeding and bad breath are all signs of gingivitis – if this sounds familiar, book an appointment with a dentist.
- We all know the drill – brush at least twice a day, and floss to break up plaque as it builds up between your teeth.
- If plaque turns into tartar, you'll need to get it scraped off by a dental hygienist.
- Don't brush too hard – overzealous cleaning can also cause damage that could allow bacteria into your bloodstream.
- Smoking makes it harder to spot signs of gum disease, such as bleeding gums, due to decreased blood flow, and harder to treat because smoking weakens the immune system – so all the more reason to quit.

Importantly, the team also found that there were signs of *P. gingivalis* in the brains of people who had not had Alzheimer's, albeit in much lower quantities. This suggested that the infection happens before the onset of the disease, and is a potential cause, rather than something that happens afterwards,[217] for instance because of people being less likely to look after their teeth when they have dementia, or because for some reason it's easier for the bacteria to enter the brains of people with Alzheimer's. People with both Alzheimer's and gum disease had previously been seen to decline faster into dementia, leading to the assumption that inflammation from the infection could be making Alzheimer's worse. But now there was evidence of direct causation. Admittedly, the study was only in fifty people, but experiments in mice lend weight to the findings. When the team mimicked gum disease in mice, *P. gingivalis* infected their brains and wreaked the same havoc, causing amyloid plaques and tau tangles, and damage to brain cells.[218]

This all fits with a previous discovery, in 2016, that amyloid can form as a defence to bacterial infection. So it seems that the hallmark signs of Alzheimer's in the brain may actually be produced in response to a gum disease infection that has travelled to the brain. And that the bacterium involved, *P. gingivalis*, also ramps up dangerous inflammation, and might also attack brain cells themselves. Animal studies also hint that infection with *P. gingivalis* can mess with the circadian clock and cause sleep disruption, which would reduce the brain's glymphatic activity – that system that clears out gunk such as amyloid while we sleep.[219]

Reversible damage

As scary as this sounds, there is some good news. A new theory of what causes Alzheimer's also offers hope of a new direction for treatment, as well as possible ways we might protect ourselves. When a drug that targeted gingipains was given to some of the mice with an infection in their brains, it soon cleared up, inflammation subsided, and levels of harmful amyloid and tau reduced. Some of the damaged neurons of the hippocampus were even restored.

When will such a treatment be available to Alzheimer's patients? Cortexyme have shown that their drug is safe in humans in initial trials, and results of a large trial on Alzheimer's patients are due out soon. Another approach underway is to develop a vaccine to prevent against gum disease in the first place.

In the meantime, we need to do all we can to look after our teeth and gums, and make regular appointments with the dentist. That's especially important given that Alzheimer's isn't the only disease thought to be influenced by gum disease. It also increases the risk of Parkinson's disease,[220] and people who have antibodies to *P. gingivalis* – a sign of having been infected – are also more likely to have a heart attack, rheumatoid arthritis or stroke. There is also a clear link between the bacterium and diabetes.

Before you panic, bear in mind that these are complex diseases with many possible causes. Gum disease is likely to be one of many contributing causes of Alzheimer's. As we've seen throughout this book, there are many factors, both genetic and to do with the way we live our lives, that play into the disease – and many of these are interconnected. Gum disease is likely to be another factor that fits the bill. It may even be the case that the very reason people with a genetic predisposition to Alzheimer's are at increased risk is because of the way *P. gingivalis* interacts with certain proteins in their body. So by all means, look after your teeth, but our quest to understand – and cure – Alzheimer's will not end in front of the bathroom mirror.

CHAPTER 27

Hearing loss is linked to dementia

Listen carefully. Of all the things that contribute to dementia, the number one risk factor we can do something about is hearing loss. Research by Frank Lin at Johns Hopkins University and his colleagues that tracked over six hundred people for around twelve years showed that mild hearing loss doubles your risk of dementia, while moderate hearing loss triples it. For those with severe hearing loss, the risk is five times as high.[221]

We don't know for certain why hearing loss increases the risk of dementia. What we do know is that our hearing tends to get worse as we age, by and large due to damage to tiny cells in the cochlea, a spiral-shaped bone in the inner ear that turns sound from vibrations in the air into electrical signals that the brain can process. Any damage means it becomes worse at encoding sounds.

Having two types of sensory impairment appears to be especially problematic. In 2021 a team of researchers in South Korea engaged more than six and a half thousand people aged fifty-eight to a hundred and one in a study for more than six years. They were asked about their vision and hearing at the start of the study and their cognitive abilities were tested every two years. Those who had both vision and hearing loss were twice as likely to go on to develop dementia than those who had just one impairment, or none, once the researchers had taken into account other factors like education and sex that impact on dementia.[222]

Brain overload

Like hearing and vision loss, dementia too becomes more common as we get older, and it could be that some of the same things as we age are responsible for all these conditions, which could explain the link. But if we look at what's going on in the brain when people become hard of hearing, it's easy to see how hearing loss itself could be the cause of dementia in some cases. If we struggle to hear sounds, we require a greater cognitive effort to process them (there's a higher cognitive load) to the detriment of other cognitive processes, such as working memory.

Another issue is that hearing is always 'switched on' whether we are tuning into it or not, so it might constantly be competing with our other mental efforts, which might in turn affect our ability to carry out all sorts of daily tasks, which is what we see with dementia.

Finally, hearing loss may also speed up brain changes involved in dementia, and people diagnosed with hearing problems tend to have shrinkage in various brain regions over the following years. The affected areas are involved not just in processing language, but also in memory, as well as areas implicated in the early stages of mild cognitive impairment (memory problems that put people at risk of going on to develop dementia) and Alzheimer's disease. And hearing loss, especially left untreated, can lead people to increased social isolation, which is yet another known risk factor for dementia.

Preventable risk

All of this is paramount because hearing loss is one of the factors contributing to dementia we can do the most about. An estimated 40 per cent of all dementia risk is preventable, according to a *Lancet* report in 2020, through such things as giving up smoking, reducing air pollution and increasing physical activity. And of these, making up 8 per cent of this preventable risk – more than any other single aspect – is hearing loss.

HOW TO PROTECT YOUR EARS FROM LOUD NOISE

At live venues:

- Give your hearing about eighteen hours to recover after a loud event such as a concert or club night.
- Don't stand near to loudspeakers.
- Take a break from the noise every fifteen minutes.
- Wear earplugs to reduce the volume.

Listening to headphones:

- If using headphones, take a five-minute break every hour.
- Use noise-cancelling headphones to block out background noise rather than just cranking up the volume.
- Only listen at 60 per cent of maximum volume or less.

In general, a noise is too loud if:

- It's over 85dB (see the diagram on page 206), especially for long timeframes.
- You have to shout over it.
- You can't hear people near to you when they talk.
- You have ringing in the ears afterwards.

And yet, of all the risk factors, hearing has probably had the least research done on it, even though it's one of the easiest to rectify, with the use of hearing aids and other therapies. Even if interventions such as these reduce only some of the cases, this could be significant given how many older adults suffer from hearing loss. The incidence of hearing problems doubles each decade, and by the age of seventy, two-thirds of people have hearing loss that affects day-to-day communication.[223]

So, what can we do about it? The most important thing is to get your hearing tested regularly as you get older, and to wear

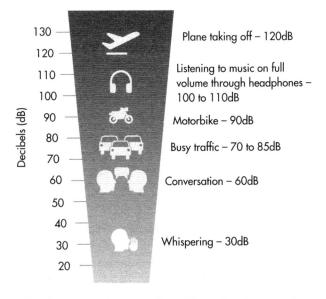

Plane taking off – 120dB

Listening to music on full
volume through headphones –
100 to 110dB

Motorbike – 90dB

Busy traffic – 70 to 85dB

Conversation – 60dB

Whispering – 30dB

Decibels (dB)

130
120
110
100
90
80
70
60
50
40
30
20

hearing aids if you need them. A 2019 study of more than
twenty-five thousand people in the US who were over fifty found
that people who wear a hearing aid for age-related hearing
problems stay sharper mentally than those who do not. And in
2021, researchers in Northern Ireland found that people with
mild cognitive impairment took on average two years longer to
develop dementia if they wore a hearing aid. It's also important
to make sure that hearing loss doesn't cause people further social
isolation, whether they have dementia or not.[224]

Early signs that you have hearing loss due to damage to the
hair cells in your ears include trouble detecting high-pitched
sounds, such as children's voices, or soft sounds like a conversation
over the phone. Tinnitus, a form of ringing in the ear, is another
giveaway. Despite the downsides of hearing loss, most people
wait on average a decade to get a hearing aid once their problems
start.[225] So if you have any of these symptoms, get your hearing
tested. It's also never too soon to start protecting your ears from
potential damage from excessive noise exposure.

PART 7

THE INFLUENCE OF YOU

By this point in the book, you will hopefully have become much better acquainted with the squidgy stuff between your ears, and how to look after it better. It almost goes without saying that the reason this is so important is because it's your brain that ultimately makes you *you*. Paradoxically, however, one problem with many of these findings is that most of the research into the brain and how to keep it ticking over healthily is conducted on large groups of people. And that's a good thing – the more people who take part in an experiment, the more significant the results are likely to be. But when we read these findings, we need to remember the very fact that our brains, their structure, the way they work, the life experiences that have shaped and sculpted them, and the genetics that underpin them, are all different. Just because researchers found a pattern when they looked at a large group of people, it doesn't necessarily mean it will be true for you – only that it was true for most of the people they looked at. To take a good example from Chapter 30, where we will look at habits, it takes on average sixty-six days to form a new habit, but some people nail it in just eighteen, whereas for others it takes the best part of a year. Scientific research can undoubtedly provide us with invaluable insights about the human brain, but it doesn't mean all of it will apply to you and your unique version.

With this in mind, in the final few chapters, we will celebrate and explore some of these differences, starting with personality. Philosophers used to think that we were born into this world a blank slate, an idea that has survived into scientific thinking until relatively recently. Today, it is more broadly acknowledged that genetics is responsible in large part for our personalities, and that this genetic predisposition interplays with our environment – ideas we explore in Chapter 28. This is important for the brain because some personality traits can put us at risk of mental-health problems, whereas others seem to be protective. Happily, we have recently discovered that personality isn't as fixed over the course of our lives as was previously thought, so there are things we can all do to improve on those aspects of our personalities that aren't so good for our mental wellbeing.

On the subject of personality, if you're the type who tends to be highly strung, you'll probably want to turn to Chapter 29, which looks at the way we respond to stress, especially in our busy lives. Here there is more good news: yes, stress can be bad for us, but you can help to protect yourself from it with the power of thought alone.

If you come to the end of this book wanting to make some positive changes, the final chapter should help. Here we'll look at what happens in the brain when we form new habits, and how to tap into that process to make better ones and lose those that do us no favours, so that you can live a more brain-healthy life with minimum effort required.

CHAPTER 28

Your personality affects your mental health

The question of where your personality comes from is a hotly debated subject. Many parents will tell you that their babies arrived in this world already equipped with some kind of innate 'temperament', rather than being a blank slate ready to be shaped exclusively by life experiences. Then there are those stories of uncanny similarities between identical twins who have been separated at birth and grew up in very different households. When they meet decades later, they wear the same clothes, and have the same interests and mannerisms. Studies comparing identical twins and fraternal twins back this up to some extent, showing that genetics clearly plays a part.

Scientists still disagree over how much of a part, however. There is no single gene for agreeableness that we can ramp up to help us make friends and influence people. Instead, many genes together will interplay with our environment to influence our personalities. Understanding this process has massive implications. It determines how much influence parents can exert over their children's behaviours, personalities and attainment, and gets to the root of big societal questions such as how much we can expect people to change and achieve. And that question of how our personalities form, and what we can do to change them, also has a lot to do with our mental wellbeing.

The big five

Given how complex personality is, it's no surprise that we don't have a perfect way to describe it, but psychologists tend to use the 'big five' system, which defines five independent personality traits, on which people sit somewhere on a sliding scale. These are openness to experience, conscientiousness, extroversion, agreeableness and neuroticism.

Using these five traits, researchers have found that our personality impacts on all aspects of success in life, from our love lives to our career prospects, our health and even longevity.[226] People who have higher conscientiousness, for example, tend to achieve better academic and professional success, better relationships and physical health. Agreeableness and extroversion have been linked to positive mental health.[227] And people who are highly open to new experiences seem to be more resilient to stress,[228] and are often good at creative thinking.

Neuroticism, however, has a worse reputation. People with this personality trait often feel overwhelmed by small setbacks and can interpret ordinary situations as threatening. With this in mind, you might not be surprised to discover that neuroticism has been linked to several mental-health conditions, including depression, eating disorders and schizophrenia.

The big five approach has come under some scrutiny, with critics arguing that it doesn't do a good enough job of encapsulating nuances in personality.

One such aspect of our characters that the big five doesn't cover, but that is increasingly drawing attention for its role in mental health, is perfectionism. While not strictly defined as a personality trait, perfectionism is described as the propensity to have overly high standards and be very self-critical, and this puts people at risk of several mental-health issues, including eating disorders, depression, anxiety and obsessive compulsive disorder.

THE BIG FIVE

The big five personality traits are a spectrum, but people who score very highly on each tend to have the following attributes:

1. Openness to experience: categorized by insight and imagination, a willingness to try new things. People who score highly for this trait tend to enjoy meeting new people, and are creative.

2. Conscientiousness: these are people who are goal orientated, thoughtful and have good impulse control. They tend to plan ahead and think about how their actions affect others.

3. Neuroticism: people with high neuroticism have elevated levels of anger, hostility, anxiety, worry, sadness, self-consciousness and vulnerability, and respond disproportionately negatively to difficult situations. They also tend to be very self-critical, are very sensitive to the criticisms of others, and often feel inadequate.

4. Extroversion: people who are highly extroverted feel energized by spending time around other people, and are very social, chatty and expressive. Conversely, those with low extroversion feel drained by social settings and dislike being the centre of attention.

5. Agreeableness: this trait is characterized by caring about others, being empathetic and kind, and wanting to help others. Highly agreeable people are also more collaborative, whereas people with low agreeableness tend to be more competitive and manipulative.

Hidden epidemic

As rates of mental-health problems are on the rise among young people in many countries, two researchers in the UK, Dr Thomas Curran and Dr Andrew Hill, wanted to find out whether a pressure for perfection might be to blame, especially given that young people today are living in a world of unprecedented scrutiny on social media, and intense pressure for academic success.

To investigate, Curran and Hill compared college students' scores on a measure of perfectionism called the Multidimensional Perfectionism Scale, between 1989 and 2016. The scale measures several different types of perfectionism: self-orientated perfectionism, which involves excessively high personal standards; society-prescribed perfectionism, which is excessively high social expectations; and other-orientated perfectionism, in which people place excessively high standards on those around them.

Looking at data from over 41,600 students in the US, Canada and the UK, Curran and Hill found that levels of all three types of perfectionism increased over time.[229] Worryingly, the biggest jump was in society-prescribed perfectionism, which is particularly bad for our mental health. This kind of perfectionism involves excessive concerns over mistakes, nagging uncertainties, fear of disapproval from others, and a big gap between self-perception and reality, and it also has the strongest link to depression, anxiety, obsessive compulsive disorder and suicide. What's more, this type of perfectionism doesn't just leave people at risk of depression, but people with depression are also at risk of developing this kind of perfectionism where they feel pressure to be perfect in the eyes of others.[230] The study has led Curran and Hill to the belief that perfectionism has become a hidden epidemic among young people.[231]

Perfectionism paradox

Paradoxically, perfectionists set themselves up for failure. Even though people with this trait do tend to be high achievers, they don't feel pleasure from reaching their goals, and instead put themselves under yet more pressure to maintain these high standards in the long term. Perfectionists obsess over any perceived inadequacies, and constantly worry about how others are viewing them. Inevitably, the quest for perfection often becomes too much, and the pressure renders them mentally unable to do their jobs, or to fulfil whatever other lofty goals they set out for themselves. Hill recently found that perfectionism among athletes, for instance, was linked to burnout, and the athletes were also more likely to suffer from burnout if they believed their coach expected perfection in others too.[232]

HOW FLAVOUR CAN CHANGE OUR PERSONALITY

For an instant boost to your sense of adventure, try chewing on some sour candy. After being made to taste one of the five different tastes – sweet, sour, bitter, salty and umami – those who had tasted something sour took bigger risks in a computer simulation directly afterwards. And, if you want to be less judgemental, put down your coffee. In another experiment, in which people were asked to judge morally dubious scenarios such as a man eating his dead dog, people who had been given a bitter drink judged the scenarios significantly more harshly than those who had consumed a drink of water.

If you're reading this and worrying that your personality might be playing havoc with your mental health, do not despair. Until relatively recently, the received wisdom was that personality developed throughout childhood and adolescence, and became fixed around the age of thirty, but we now know this isn't the case, and our personalities continue to change as we age. The most compelling study, of over 135,000 adults of different ages who completed a 'big five' personality questionnaire online, found that we tend to chill out as we age, with levels of agreeableness and conscientiousness increasing. Neuroticism declined in women, but not men, as they got older.[233] We don't know exactly what causes the change, but it could be due to modifications in the structure of the brain with age. The genetic influence on neuroticism, for instance, seems to peak in adolescence, indicating that we might be more suggestible to interventions that change our personality later in life.

It's not just age that changes us. Life events, too, can influence our personalities. For a start, new romantic relationships decrease neuroticism. When women get divorced they seem to become more extroverted and open to new experiences. And researchers in Germany have recently discovered that when we become parents, women tend to become more extroverted and agreeable, and men become less extroverted but more conscientious.[234] Unemployment is predictably bad news for personality – it makes people less agreeable and less conscientious. All that might sound a bit obvious, but it certainly challenges the idea that we are stuck with the personalities we entered adulthood with.

Personality transplant

If we can change our personalities, it might make sense for doctors to routinely screen people for personality traits that put them at risk of health problems, and take steps to intervene. Certain drugs, as well as cognitive behavioural therapy, are two things that have both been shown to reduce levels of neuroticism in people who are already being treated for specific mental-health issues.

What about the rest of us? When asked, the vast majority of people say they'd like to tweak their personalities to have a bit more of the good stuff and a little less angst. And you don't need to have a baby or go through a divorce to change your score on the big five personality traits. Psychotherapy and psychedelic drugs can both reduce levels of neuroticism and increase openness,[235] but there are simpler ways, too.

One of these is to identify specific behaviours that reflect the personality change you'd like to see in yourself. When people were asked to jot down these behaviours as part of an intervention, they reported significant changes in their personality four months later. The key was to be specific with these actions. The technique did not work when people wrote down vague goals like 'I will be more organized', or 'I will talk to more people'. Instead, try using 'if x then y' language – for example, 'If I disagree with something in class, I will voice my opinion.'[236]

THE ORIGINS OF PERSONALITY

What shapes our personalities? Genes certainly play a part. A recent study found that there are over six hundred separate genes involved in neuroticism, and that they seemed to contribute towards two distinct versions of the personality trait – one that tended towards more depressive mood, and the other towards more worrying.[237] But even if we can identify genes that are involved in personality, the fact there are so many and that each plays a relatively small part shows how complex these traits are. Besides, these genes only account for a small amount in the difference between people's personalities – environment plays a huge role too. One especially powerful environmental factor is the kind of parenting we grew up with. Overly punitive parenting seems to lead to perfectionist traits, for instance. Children's early tendencies, their equivalent of personality, can be shaped by the kinds of friendships they make at school. And far from being fixed throughout our lives, our personalities are increasingly being shown to be malleable at the hands of our life experiences.

Admittedly, the volunteers in this study were rating their own change in personality, so there's a chance they might be biased or misguided. But last year, researchers in the US and Switzerland conducted a randomized controlled trial to see whether they could use a smartphone app to coach people into changing their personalities, with the app delivering tools and techniques to help them reach their goals. After three months, volunteers who used the app saw significant changes in their personality compared to people who were on the waiting list to use it, and the effects lasted for at least three months after the experiment ended. What's more, close friends, family and intimate partners also agreed that the volunteers' personalities had made the desired shift.

Overall, people who took part in the study found it easier to make a positive shift towards adopting a new personality trait, rather than reducing their levels of traits they didn't like,[238] so if you want to elicit change, this could be a good place to start. And the effort should pay off – managing to shift personality in line with our goals has been shown to improve mental wellbeing,[239] so there's everything to play for.

Perfectionism too, can be helped with cognitive behavioural therapy.[240] And parents and teachers can play a role in trying to reduce perfectionism in the next generation. We know that overly critical parenting styles that focus on achievement can promote perfectionism, and parents who feel pressure to be perfect should be cautious about that anxiety rubbing off on their children. In the classroom there are plenty of things that can reduce the pressure on children to achieve a perfect performance, for instance focusing on overall progress rather than picking up on unimportant mistakes, setting obtainable goals based on the abilities of the individual, and making sure that rewards and sanctions are private, so as to reduce feelings of shame and guilt.[241] All of this should help set children up for success in their endeavours, rather than already striving for the impossible.

PERSONALITY-CHANGING GOALS

If you want to change your personality, one experiment showed that it helps to have specific goals in mind. The researchers put together a list of goals for each personality type, some of which are listed below. Choose as many as you like, or make up your own, but be precise about the actions you will take.

To be more extroverted:
- Take decisions in groups more often.
- Be more enterprising.
- Be less quiet.

To be more agreeable:
- Be more polite and less harsh.
- Appreciate others more.
- Treat others with respect.

To be more conscientious:
- Be less messy.
- Procrastinate less.
- Stay on a task until it's done.

To be less neurotic:
- Worry less often.
- Be more self-confident.
- Be less moody.

To be more open:
- Be more enthusiastic about new things.
- Be more curious.
- Question routines and traditions more often.

CHAPTER 29

Stress doesn't have to be bad

If you've ever tried laughter yoga, the chances are it started off pretty awkwardly. It tends to involve standing around with a group of strangers, staring them in the eyes and making voluntary laughing sounds. With none of the usual social cues and feel-good factor associated with humour, the whole thing can feel a little uncomfortable. And yet after a few rounds of highly embarrassing 'ho ho ho, ha ha ha, hi hi hi's, something strange starts to happen. All that surreal awkwardness makes it impossible to keep a straight face, the embarrassment melts away and before you know it, you're in fits of genuine giggles with all the psychological benefits spontaneous laughter brings.

What has any of this got to do with stress? Well, learning to be more humorous is more than a passing yoga trend – it is one of many ways that we might be able to protect ourselves against the effects of stress, to learn to keep our cool in the face of adversity, and make ourselves more resilient.

Stress is a growing health problem and has been linked to all six of the main causes of death in the West – cancer, heart disease, liver disease, accidents, lung disease and suicide.[242] It can weaken the immune system, leaving us more prone to infection and reducing the effectiveness of vaccines. Stress can also mess with our gut, as we discovered in Chapter 1, causing it to become more 'leaky' and allowing bacteria to enter the bloodstream and trigger inflammation. Things don't look much better when we turn to the brain. Stress causes a reduction in cognitive performance and productivity, and increased mental-health problems including depression – even the anticipation of stress can lower our cognitive abilities.[243] And stress forces us to focus on what's directly in front of us, rather than seeing the bigger picture. On top of all that, it messes with our relationships too, and compels us to make choices that can themselves be bad for our health, such as smoking and eating unhealthily. All of which has led the World Health Organization to describe it as the 'epidemic of the twenty-first century'.

What is stress?

All the more surprising, then, that stress is designed to save our life, not shorten it. All the sensations you feel when you are stressed – increased heart rate, sweaty palms, a sudden surge of energy and even tummy trouble – are a result of a finely tuned set of processes that start in the brain and are intended to keep us safe from potential threats. As we've heard elsewhere in this book, the amygdala is the brain's fear centre, and it is constantly primed to detect threats in our environment. If it deems something to be of concern, it flags it up via the hypothalamus, which triggers our flight or fight response. The hormone adrenaline courses through the body, and blood flow increases, which boosts alertness and primes us to run. The release of another hormone, cortisol, makes sure that this stress response continues as long as it needs to, releasing stored glucose to give us more energy, and dampening down other bodily processes like digestion and the immune system so that everything can focus on the threat in front of us.

Clearly then, stress in the right situation can be a lifesaver, and can also be helpful in daily life to get us through important jobs and challenges. But yet again, problems arise when this system remains switched on for too long, is triggered by things that aren't really a threat, or is inappropriately strong, any of which can lead to myriad health problems.

The good news is that even if stress on some level is ubiquitous in our busy lives, not everyone responds to it in the same way, and the way we do respond can determine how badly it affects our health. Even better, recent research shows us how we can harness the power of stress as a force for good, and turn it to our advantage.

Most of us know someone who never seems to crumble under pressure, who rarely lets a stressful situation get to them. Scientists have been keen to understand why some people fare better when they are stressed, otherwise known as resilience, not least because understanding these individual differences could help decide who is best suited to high-risk jobs such as in military special forces, or firefighting, where the intense stress can leave some employees with mental-health problems.

The root of resilience

Part of the answer comes down to early life experiences. Studies of Romanian orphans who were either adopted at a young age or stayed in the care system for a long time have shown how early-life hardship can impact on the brain in this important period for forming new connections, leaving people at higher risk of PTSD and depression later in life. These brain changes also blunt the stress response, causing those who stayed in care to produce less cortisol in stressful situations – in other words, an inappropriate stress response. Conversely, having strong, stable and supportive relationships when we are growing up can help to buffer against stressful events later in life.

Another key factor in how we all respond to stress is a brain chemical called Neuropeptide Y (NPY), which helps control stress and emotional behaviours. Studies of the military have found that, compared to regular soldiers, those in the special forces had a better-tuned NPY system, and that the more of the chemical they produced, the better they fared mentally in different situations. Because NPY acts as an on–off switch for stress, it seems this system could be stopping people from having an overly strong stress response, and is also stopping this response from remaining switched on and leading to chronic stress. Although our NPY response has a strong genetic component,[244] it's not totally fixed and there is tentative research that mindfulness can help to improve it.

Your personality, too, plays a role in your resilience to stress. In a research study aptly titled 'Is humour the best medicine?', Michael Sliter at Indiana University–Purdue University Indianapolis found that firefighters who used humour as a coping mechanism were less likely to experience burnout and PTSD after traumatic experiences on the job.[245] Humour is a particularly appealing method of countering stress because it not only protects against its negative effects, but has been proven to have lots of positive effects on our wellbeing, too.

Not everyone is naturally jolly in the face of adversity though. Is there hope for them? Scientists think so, with preliminary studies showing that several weeks of humour training, which included laughter exercises and a session on telling jokes, can help people to learn how to use humour as a coping strategy, and the training resulted in a decrease in perceived stress, anxiety and depressiveness.[246] Another recent study found the frequency of laughter in our lives is more important than the intensity when it comes to buffering against stress.[247]

Rethinking stress

If you still can't fathom the thought of laughter yoga or humour training, a simple trick of the mind could be even more beneficial. While there's incontrovertible evidence that stress, especially chronic, prolonged stress, can be bad for body and mind, whether it is bad for you or not could have a lot to do with how you think about it. This is what researchers call your 'stress mindset', and adopting the right one could do more than protect you from the negative effects of stress – it could even make stress something that's actually good for you.

From what you've read so far in this chapter, and the way stress is generally negatively portrayed, you are likely to have what researchers call a 'stress-is-debilitating' mindset. But stress doesn't have to be bad. The stress response that primes us for getting out of danger is also useful for productivity – with stress hormones improving our attention and memory. It makes us instantly more alert. Our brain is sharper under pressure.

MIND OVER MATTER

The right mindset isn't just important in stress, it can have a profound impact on other areas of life too. Ageing is one of them. People who view ageing in a negative light tend to adopt fewer healthy behaviours and are less likely to visit the doctor. As a result, they age worse and die sooner. Our intellect is also subject to how we view it: students who view intelligence as something that is malleable and can be worked on, rather than something fixed and genetically determined, feel more motivated, get better scores and enjoy learning more. Most spectacularly, the benefits of exercise, too, are at the mercy of our mindsets. Hotel workers who considered their job to be good exercise lost more weight and had higher improvements in blood pressure than those who did the same work but didn't consider it to be good exercise. And people who think they are drinking a high-calorie milkshake feel fuller than those who believe it to be a low-calorie version.

On top of that, even long-term stress can have surprisingly positive effects on the body. Because stress is telling our body to prepare for potential damage, the hormones it produces can rebuild cells and make new proteins, the body's building blocks, as well as priming our immune system, leaving us in better physical shape. Studies in mice found that stress boosted neurogenesis in the hippocampus and improved cognitive skills. And a recent study showed that in healthy children with supportive parents, some stress early in life can be good for a child's brain development.[248] What's more, while it's true that stress can be detrimental to our relationships, those of us who have been through a stressful experience and come out the other side often do so feeling mentally tougher, having built strong new friendships, and with a renewed sense of appreciation for the good things in our lives.

What should we make of this apparent 'stress paradox'? The simple answer is, focus on the good stuff. The more people adopt a mindset that stress can be beneficial, the less negative effects of stress they tend to experience, and the more benefits stress brings. It's a self-fulfilling prophecy.

If you're not convinced, take one study which found that if a doctor told people who had a mild allergic reaction that it would get better, the symptoms improved faster than for those in another group who were simply examined by a doctor. And one study of thirty thousand people showed that when people had a lot of stress but believed it was good for them, it had fewer negative health implications than in people who had less stress but believed it was bad for them (worst of all is to have a lot of stress and believe it's bad for you). People who view stress as something enhancing, rather than debilitating, also have a more moderate cortisol response when they are placed in a stressful situation.[249]

The power of positive thinking

How easy is it to switch to a different stress mindset? To find out, Professor Alia Crum at Yale University and her colleagues assigned office workers into one of two groups. One group watched short videos that told them how stress is bad, and that it can cause workplace mistakes and illness. The other group learned that stress improves workplace performance, immunity and wellbeing. After a week, the training successfully changed people's mindsets. Even better, those who now believed stress to be beneficial suffered fewer negative effects of stress.[250] Simply believing stress was good protected them from it.

This is just one study of many showing that people who believe stress is good for them have better mental health, are more productive at work and have a better-tuned physiological stress response in stressful situations. They are also more open to feedback, which can help them grow and improve.

Crum says that there are three simple steps we can take to turn stress to our advantage.

The first is to name it – for instance, 'I'm stressed that I'm not going to meet my book deadline.' Naming your stress is useful because it moves the reaction in your brain from the amygdala, which is more emotive and reactionary, to the prefrontal cortex involved in more deliberate thinking and planning, which means you are then better able to tackle the issue rationally. Here, mindfulness techniques can help you to become more in tune with your response to stress – for instance whether you become defensive, or start snacking. Increased awareness will help you recognize and deal with it.

The second step to turning stress into a positive is to 'own' your stress. This means acknowledging that the reason we get stressed about things is that we care about them, which is actually rather positive. It's a reminder that you're on a journey towards something you want, and that it's not always easy to get there. So in my case – this stress will help me meet my book deadline, which is something I want to achieve and I knew was never going to be easy. It won't make the stress go away, but owning the stress in this way might make it easier to deal with and to view it as something necessary to experience for a greater goal.

HOW TO BE LESS STRESSED

- Listen to music – it can lower levels of stress hormones (for more on the benefits of music, see Chapter 19).
- Get moving – exercise helps to lower our perception of stress.
- Meditate – the practice can help us to control emotions better and be more resilient to stress.
- Get some rest – lack of sleep affects our emotions, leaving us with a shorter fuse and finding it harder to deal with difficult situations.
- Invest in your social networks – they are one of the best ways to be resilient to stressful situations, possibly because they trigger feel-good chemicals like oxytocin in the brain.
- Make sure you are rewarded for your work – a study on workplace stress found that people who work hard and aren't recognized for it are at greater risk of stress and burnout.

Finally, you need to try and use your stress response to your benefit. After all, what happens in our body when we are stressed evolved to help us deal with life-or-death situations. The effect on us physiologically is better focus, a rush of energy, and more alertness – abilities we often strive for at other times. So, in my example, better focus is very helpful for writing. The stress response also helps cells to repair and grow, and gives us an immune boost ready for that impending attack. The key to this strategy is to think about the stress response in positive terms. Reframing anxiety as excitement has been shown to help people do better in tests, negotiations and public speaking.

All this goes to show that if you can think of stress through a lens that depicts it as something that can be beneficial, rather than something that is always detrimental, you could reap all sorts of benefits, not least a better physiological response to the stress itself. It's time to stop stressing about stress.

CHAPTER 30

How to form healthy habits

Throughout this book, we've discovered the myriad ways, from diet through exercise, mental workouts, self-care and more that we can keep our brains healthy and our minds feeling good. Now it's time to put that knowledge into practice. Some of these things will be easy to achieve; if you already own a pet, love walks in nature, gorge on fresh berries and love the taste of dark chocolate, you can smugly celebrate the habits you already enjoy that are also beneficial for the brain. But if you're reading this book, the chances are you aren't already living the perfect brain-healthy lifestyle (and if you are, remember perfectionism isn't all it's cracked up to be!). We all know that forming good habits and breaking the bad can be difficult. But here, neuroscience can help too.

A lot of what we do in our daily lives – as much as 40 per cent, according to one oft-cited study[251] – is done on autopilot. Imagine a train journey to a new job. On that first day, you'll need to find out what time the train leaves, which platform to wait on, how many stops to go and which one to get off at, as well as the right exit out of the station and then the new walk to the office at the other end. You might also need to remember a key code to get into the building, and think about which floor to press in the elevator. In the first few days, you'll need to give a lot of conscious thought to that journey, which will require hard work by your prefrontal cortex, an area of the brain that plays an important role in impulse control, planning, decision making and attention. To turn these thoughts into actions, the prefrontal cortex will communicate with other areas of the brain, one of the most important for habit formation being the striatum, deep in the brain, which is involved in mood, reward and movement.[252] Drawing on past memories and instructions from the prefrontal cortex, the striatum will signal to your muscles what to do to carry out the necessary actions.

Switching to autopilot

Give it a few weeks, however, and the journey to work will become second nature. You might even turn up at the office one day to find that you spent the entire way there thinking about your weekend plans and that, try as you might, you can't even remember details from the trip, like where you stood on the platform or how busy the train was. This is because with repetition, the prefrontal cortex needs to do less and less work to make the behaviour happen, passing the baton to the striatum, which you could consider the brain's autopilot.[253] When we repeat a behaviour, studies in animals show that the brain waves in the striatum become slower and more in sync, presumably a hallmark that the habit has formed.[254] After this point, the striatum seems to be able to pull the trigger on rewarding behaviours, telling the body what to do, without the cognitive input from your thinking brain.

The striatum also plays a role in what scientists call 'chunking' of behaviour when habits form. When you put your shoes on to leave the house, you are really doing lots of little actions. Picking up your shoe, putting it on your foot, putting one lace over the other to tie the knot and so on. Chunking allows your brain to package those actions into one single habit – putting your shoes on – to spare you the agony of thinking about each step.

Experiments that look at brain activity in rodents once they have learned a new habit, such as how to find their way through a maze to reach a reward, show a flurry of brain cells firing in the striatum at the beginning and at the end of the new behaviour.[255] As one of the key researchers in this field, Professor Anne Graybiel, explains, it's as if the brain is packaging up the behaviour, so from start to end it can run automatically. Another way to think about it is that the behaviour is put into brackets, with the activity of the striatum signalling the start and finish.

The power of habit

Habit formation makes perfect sense – if we had to consciously think about every aspect of our day, from remembering where we keep the coffee in the kitchen, to the route to work, and how to tie our laces, the brain would soon become overloaded and we wouldn't have the capacity to think about much else. Once a behaviour is chunked, the striatum can press play and off we go. So, shortcutting to habitual behaviours is incredibly useful and efficient, but – in the context of bad habits – can also be our downfall, because once they get into this automatic mode, it's much harder to interrupt them. Given this, how can we tap into these processes to help us form better habits, and snap out of the bad ones?

To start, it helps to think about what a habit really is. Habits don't exist on their own; they are tightly connected to cues in our environment. In fact, scientists define habits as a mental association between a cue and a behaviour where, through repetition, people feel an impulse to act out the behaviour when they encounter that cue. If you start removing your shoes as soon as you enter the house, before too long you'll do this automatically – the cue is entering the house, the behaviour or habit is taking your shoes off. Or you might habitually reach for something sweet after a meal – the end of the meal is the trigger, rather than your appetite. Think about your day and you might be surprised just how many little habits like this you actually have.

HOW TO ACHIEVE LONG-TERM GOALS

The brain focuses on the present moment and links our sense of self to the here and now, whereas it sees the future you as more of a stranger, a fact that has been borne out in experiments using brain scans. That makes it particularly hard to act on long-term plans. Some people try to visualize their long-term goal, such as what they would look like on their wedding day, to stay focused on a diet or exercise regime. But science suggests this might be misguided. When people visualize this kind of success story, it actually tricks the brain into feeling like it's already achieved the goal, loosening the resolve needed to get there. A better approach is to think about a worst-case scenario – not fitting into that expensive wedding dress, say – a way of thinking known as 'defensive pessimism', to keep the mission on track.[256]

The fact that habits are tightly connected to our environment gives us the first insight into how to make and break them. Where we are, who we are with and what we are doing are all cues that can trigger specific habitual behaviours.

One way to hijack the system is to capitalize on big changes in our environment, such as going on holiday or starting a new job. At these times it will be easier to break old habits and form new ones because we will have a fresh set of routines and will have left behind many of the old cues.

The next step is to link the new behaviours you want to turn into habits to a specific part of your routine or a time of day. If, for example, you want to start eating a more gut-friendly diet, you might decide to sprinkle berries and seeds on top of your morning oatmeal – something you already eat by force of habit. Or leave a note on the coffee machine to drink a glass of water before your daily morning Joe. Before long, you will no longer need the note. Piggybacking new habits onto existing parts of our routine gives us the cues our brain needs to eventually make that behaviour an automatic one.

To maximize those chances, it helps to be as specific as you can. So rather than deciding to 'eat more vegetables', try saying 'I will eat more vegetables for lunch'. One proven way to get specific and boost habit formation is to use 'if–then' plans. 'If I go to the kitchen, I will drink a glass of water,' for example. This helps to make the behaviour automatic, and bypass the need for conscious thought and self-control.

As well as being specific, you should be realistic with your goals. So if you want to do more yoga, try spending ten minutes on the mat every day after you wake up, rather than trying to do three longer sessions at some point during the week. Once daily yoga is a habit, you can increase the length. Time cues can also work – for instance, you might take your omega oil supplement at 9 a.m. each day. A study in 2021 found that it didn't matter whether the cue came from your routine or was a specific time of the day. The cue is the important thing.

Early bird …

That said, morning might turn out to be the ideal time to form a new habit, according to a study in which a small group of students were asked to do a short hip-flexor stretch either first thing in the morning or last thing before bed for ninety days. The habit began to be automatic much faster for the morning stretchers, who were on track to have it become second nature by 100 days compared to 150 for the evening group.[257] The key seems to have been that levels of the stress hormone cortisol, which is known to be involved in learning new behaviours, tends to be higher in the morning than in the evening. The fact that cortisol levels differ in the day from person to person could also help explain why some people find it harder than others to stick to their habits.

Whatever the time of day, repetition really is key with habit formation, especially in the early days. Study after study shows that when people are successful at forming new habits, it's the first few times that the behaviour is carried out that play the biggest role in making it automatic. As time goes on, each repeated behaviour makes a bit less of a difference until it reaches a plateau – at which point the habit is formed, and you enter maintenance mode. Not all habits last, but by their very nature, once they are automatic, it's much harder to break them (as we all know from our bad habits). The key is to be regular and consistent.

If you do fall off the wagon, however, don't give up. It can take a long time to form a new habit, so the odd mistake is no big deal. One study from 2009 asked almost a hundred people to try and form a new eating, drinking or behaviour-based habit. It took them on average sixty-six days to form the new habit, but the time varied wildly between the participants, taking some as little as eighteen days and others as many as two hundred and fifty-four.[258] Importantly, the odd slip-up didn't seem to matter. Similarly, much more recent research found it took fifty-nine days on average to form a habit, backing up the idea that you should stay with it for a couple of months at least. Encouragingly, repetition seems to be a lot more important than self-control for making habits stick.[259]

Breaking bad

How about breaking bad habits? In 2018, Graybiel's team discovered that as well as the neurons in the striatum that fire in sync at the start and end of a habit, there is another set that fire in the middle. Called interneurons, these inhibit other neurons from firing, presumably to prevent a new routine from starting until this one has run its course.[260] Together, this clever system makes it very hard to break a habit once it has formed. Fortunately, even once it has passed control over to the striatum, the prefrontal cortex still keeps a watchful eye on proceedings and can cut in, in case of an emergency.

HOW TO HACK YOUR HABITS

- If you are trying to exert self-control, have a full bladder. People taking part in a study were able to show more self-control – opting to wait for a bigger reward rather than receiving instant gratification – when they had drunk lots of water some time before. It seems that self-control in one area of our bodies can extend to others too.

- If you want more willpower, the trick is to convince yourself you have more. People who believe willpower is limited give up sooner on tasks than people who believe it is potentially limitless and the more we exert it, the more we get. They also eat more healthily, and do better in exams.

- Change your environment to make brain-healthy habits easier. For instance, filling the fridge with berries and stocking dark chocolate rather than the milkier kinds. You might still be reaching for a snack, but you'll only have the best options on offer.

- Stress interferes with habit formation by boosting the sense of reward we get from the striatum, and reducing the self-control exerted by the prefrontal cortex. Together, this is a recipe for reaching for a short-term treat rather than a long-term goal. So for the best chance of forming healthy habits, keep stress levels down. All the more reason not to beat yourself up if you fall off the wagon.

- If you're trying to break a bad habit, keep a diary of all the times you do this negative thing. This accountability will help to bring that unconscious action into the forefront of your thinking mind, helping your prefrontal cortex back to exert more control over your actions.

So if you really want to break bad habits, the trick is to become more consciously aware of them so that eventually this thinking part of the brain kicks in again. One way is to make a note in a diary each time you do the undesirable behaviour. The more attention you pay to it, the better your chances of switching off autopilot. If that sounds too much like hard work, you could always try and swap some brain-healthier choices into your old habits. If you can't resist a tipple in the evening, for instance, make it a red wine. Or switch milk chocolate for dark in your morning snack.

Perhaps the best advice is to start with those brain-boosting habits you think you'll love. Not all habits are equal when it comes to how hard they are to make or break, and behaviours that trigger a big hit to the brain's reward pathways, such as eating calorie-rich food, will form more easily and be harder to undo. People in the research who succeeded in forming a new habit tended to be those who had chosen a behaviour that was intrinsically more rewarding to them. So if you are trying to build a brain-healthy behaviour into your life, the best thing to do is pick something you think you'll enjoy.[261]

Conclusion

My two grandmothers were formidable women who lived well into their nineties, both staying in their own homes and remaining lucid right up until the final days. Despite my work as a science journalist, writing and editing countless articles about the effect of our daily lives on the brain, I've always had a sense of smugness about my own future in this respect. I considered myself lucky: my grandmothers must have been dealt a good hand when it came to genes – genes I must have inherited. Having won this genetic jackpot, all I had to do was sit back and enjoy my ticket to long life.

If you've read this far, you'll know this is wishful thinking. It goes against all the latest evidence on the importance of our lifestyle choices in relation to long-term brain health, and it also does a disservice to the way my grandmothers chose to live their lives.

The two women were very different. One was French, drank red wine like it was going out of fashion, was tough and pragmatic, and never married, living most of her life on her own. My English grandma was married for over fifty years, surrounded herself with family, and was emotional and warm. I've always considered them chalk and cheese. But this book has got me noticing the similarities between them, too. Both were fiercely social, they enjoyed travel, and learned languages. They both worked, but after retirement age kept mentally and socially busy, volunteering, learning new hobbies, travelling.

Is it good genes that my grandmothers were dealt? Or was

it the way they lived? Of course the answer is both, especially given our growing awareness of how lifestyle factors like diet and exercise can switch genes on and off. Being dealt a good hand helps, but it's just the start. Hopefully I'll find out the answer in the decades to come, but I'm not going to wait until then to take action.

This is one of the most important things I hope this book has highlighted: when it comes to the ageing brain, the time to start making changes is today, here and now, regardless of how old you are. Learning about some of the incredible discoveries I have documented in this book has caused me to make many small changes in my own life that I hope will make a difference. I'm spending more time outdoors, in particular choosing to exercise in nature rather than in the gym. I've invested in a lamp that switches to warm red light in the evening, and bright blue light in the day, to help keep my body clock in sync. And I've ditched short-term fad diets for fibre-rich food that will nurture my microbiome.

This brings me to the important takeaway: healthy brain ageing means playing the long game, making the right choices day in, day out. There's no twelve-week plan, and you can't post the results on Instagram. That doesn't mean it has to be boring. My grandmothers knew nothing about this research, but they did things they enjoyed. Learning about jazz at the University of the Third Age. Riding through Yemen on a yak. Find things you love now, and enjoy the brain-boosting benefits later.

And these kinds of personal choices are just the start. As we discover more and more about the vital role of our lifestyles on our mental and brain health, the issue shifts from personal action to the way we function as a society. The medical profession is increasingly catching on to the importance of lifestyle factors in preventing cognitive decline and protecting our mental health, and there is now a growing movement of lifestyle medicine, which looks at how things such as exercise, diet and sleep can keep us well.

As a society, it is more important than ever that everyone has access to the same opportunities to cash in on these benefits, whether that's all schoolchildren getting enough exercise to benefit their learning and mental health, or older adults having the social support they need to protect them from the effects of loneliness.

We must also get better at talking about mental health and giving people the tools to nurture this body–mind connection. And it must become acceptable to prioritise things like sleep and social contact when we require them. They shouldn't be seen as frivolous luxuries, but as key to our long-term health. I would suggest that it's time to think of these kinds of activities as a sort of social vaccine against illness – one that will benefit us not just as individuals, but as a wider society too.

Endnotes

Introduction

1 De Lucia, C., et al. (2020), 'Lifestyle mediates the role of nutrient-sensing pathways in cognitive aging: Cellular and epidemiological evidence', *Nature Communications*.

2 Miquel, S., et al. (2018), 'Poor cognitive ageing: Vulnerabilities, mechanisms and the impact of nutritional interventions', *Ageing Research Reviews*.

3 Hiddenhearing.co.uk (2020), 'Address a hearing loss to keep your brain sharp'.

PART 1: DIET
Introduction

4 GBD 2017 Diet Collaborators (2019), 'Health effects of dietary risks in 195 countries, 1990–2017: A systematic analysis for the Global Burden of Disease Study 2017', *The Lancet*.

1: What to eat to boost your mood

5 Bonaz, B., et al. (2018), 'The vagus nerve at the interface of the microbiota–gut–brain axis', *Frontiers in Neuroscience*.

6 Mayer, E. (2016), *The Mind–Gut Connection*.

7 Rossi, M. (2019), 'Nutrition: An old science in a new microbial light', *Nutritional Bulletin*.

8 Xue, R., et al. (2018), 'Peripheral dopamine controlled by gut microbes inhibits invariant natural killer T cell-mediated hepatitis', *Frontiers in Immunology*.

9 Sudo, N, et al. (2004), 'Postnatal microbial colonization programs the hypothalamic-pituitary-adrenal system for stress response in mice', *Journal of Physiology*.

10 Fda.org (2020), 'Fecal microbiota for transplantation: Safety alert – risk of serious adverse events likely due to transmission of pathogenic organisms'.

11 Dinan, T. (2013), 'Microbiome, brain and behavior', *National Human Genome Institute Lecture*.

12 Tillisch, K., et al. (2017), 'Brain structure and response to emotional stimuli as related to gut microbial profiles in healthy women', *Psychosomatic Medicine*.

13 *New Scientist* (2019), 'How what you eat directly influences your mental health'.

14 Rossi, Dr M. (2019), *Eat Yourself Healthy*.

15 Van de Wouw, M., et al. (2018), 'Short-chain fatty acids: Microbial metabolites that alleviate stress-induced brain–gut axis alterations', *Psychosomatic Medicine*.

2: Going hungry could keep your brain young

16 Vauzour, D., et al. (2016), 'Nutrition for the ageing brain: Towards evidence for an optimal diet', *Ageing Research Reviews*.

17 Brainfacts.org (2018), 'How does fasting affect the brain?'

18 Mattson, M. (2021), 'How brain & body adapt to intermittent bioenergetic challenge', I ÄGHE Fasting Congress.

19 The *Observer* (2013), 'How to live longer – the experts' guide to ageing'.

20 Kim, C., et al. (2020), 'Energy restriction enhances adult hippocampal neurogenesis-associated memory after four weeks in an adult human population with central obesity: A randomized controlled trial', *Nutrients*.

21 Mattson, M. (2021), 'How brain & body adapt to intermittent bioenergetic challenge', I ÄGHE Fasting Congress.

3: The promise of brain-boosting foods

22 Wang, D., et al. (2021), 'The gut microbiome modulates the protective association between a Mediterranean diet and cardiometabolic disease risk', *Nature Medicine*.

23 Psaltopoulou, T., et al. (2013), 'Mediterranean diet, stroke, cognitive impairment, and depression: A meta-analysis', *Annals of Neurology*.

24 Jacka, F., et al. (2011), 'The association between habitual diet quality and the common mental disorders in community-dwelling adults: The Hordaland Health study', *Psychosomatic Medicine*.

25 Stahl, S., et al. (2014), 'Coaching in healthy dietary practices in at-risk older adults: A case of indicated depression prevention', *American Journal of Psychiatry*. Retrieved via foodandmoodcentre.com.au/2016/07/diet-and-mental-health/.

26 Jacka, F., et al. (2017), 'A randomised controlled trial of dietary improvement for adults with major depression (the 'SMILES' trial)', *BMC Medicine*.

27 KimberlyWilson.co (2017), 'Treating Depression with Diet: The "SMILES" Trial'.

28 Francis, H., et al. (2019), 'A brief diet intervention can reduce symptoms of depression in young adults – a randomised controlled trial', PLOS One.

29 Mosconi, Dr L. (2018), *Brain food: How to Eat Smart and Sharpen Your Mind*.

30 Chang, S.-C., et al. (2016), 'Dietary flavonoid intake and risk of incident depression in midlife and older women', *American Journal of Clinical Nutrition*.

31 Letteneur, L., et al. (2017), 'Flavonoid intake and cognitive decline over a 10-year period', *American Journal of Epidemiology*.

32 foodandmoodcentre.com.au (no date available), 'Diet and mental health'.

4: Alzheimer's could be the diabetes of the brain

33 *New Scientist* (2013), 'Are Alzheimer's and diabetes the same disease?'

34 Lin, X., et al. (2020), 'Global, regional, and national burden and trend of diabetes in 195 countries and territories: An analysis from 1990 to 2025', *Scientific Reports*.

35 *New Scientist* (2012), 'Food for thought: Eat your way to dementia'.

36 Athauda, D., et al. (2017), 'Exenatide once weekly versus placebo in Parkinson's disease: A randomised, double-blind, placebo-controlled trial', *The Lancet.*

37 Chohan, H., et al. (2021), 'Type 2 diabetes as a determinant of Parkinson's disease risk and progression', *Movement Disorders.*

PART 2: SLEEP
5: Sleeping on it improves learning and memory

38 Tononi, G. (2009), 'Slow wave homeostasis and synaptic plasticity. *Journal of Clinical Sleep Medicine.*

39 Lockley, S. and Foster, R. (2012), *Sleep: A Very Short Introduction*, Oxford.

40 Koudier, S., Andrillon, T., et al. (2014), 'Inducing task-relevant responses to speech in the sleeping brain', *Cell.*

41 Paller, K., Creery, J. and Schechtman, E. (2021), 'Memory and sleep: How sleep cognition can change the waking mind for the better', *Annual Reviews.*

42 Arzi, A., Holtzman, Y., et al. (2014), 'Olfactory aversive conditioning during sleep reduces cigarette-smoking behavior', *Journal of Neuroscience.*

6: The truth about sleep and Alzheimer's

43 Mander, B., Marks, S., et al. (2015), 'β-amyloid disrupts human NREM slow waves and related hippocampus-dependent memory consolidation', *Nature Neuroscience.*

44 Kang, J.-E., Lim, M., et al. (2009), 'Amyloid-beta dynamics are regulated by orexin and the sleep–wake cycle', *Science.*

45 Ju, Y.-E., Ooms, S., et al. (2017), 'Slow wave sleep disruption increases cerebrospinal fluid amyloid-β levels', *Brain.*

46 Holth, J., et al. (2019), 'The sleep–wake cycle regulates brain interstitial fluid tau in mice and CSF tau in humans', *Science*; and Lucey, B., et al. (2019), 'Reduced non-rapid eye movement sleep is associated with tau pathology in early Alzheimer's disease', *Science Translational Medicine.*

47 *New Scientist* (2017), 'Wake-up call: How a lack of sleep can cause Alzheimer's'.

48 Xie, L., Kang, H., Chen, M., et al. (2013), 'Sleep drives metabolite clearance from the adult brain', *Science.*

49 Npr.org (2019), 'How deep sleep may help the brain clear Alzheimer's toxins'.

50 Winer, J., Mander, B., Jagust, W. and Walker, M. (2021), 'Sleep disturbance is associated with longitudinal Aβ accumulation in healthy older adults', *Alzheimer's & Dementia.*

51 *New Scientist* (2017), 'Wake-up call: How a lack of sleep can cause Alzheimer's'.

52 Cordone, S., Scarpelli, S., et al. (2021), 'Sleep-based interventions in Alzheimer's disease: Promising approaches from prevention to treatment along the disease trajectory', *Pharmaceuticals.*

53 Westerberg, C., et al. (2015), 'Memory improvement via slow-oscillatory stimulation during sleep in older adults', *Neurobiology of Ageing.*

54 Basedovsky, L., et al. (2017), 'Auditory closed-loop stimulation of EEG slow

oscillations strengthens sleep and signs of its immune-supportive function', *Nature Communications*.

55 Ma, Y., Liang, L. and Zheng, F. (2020), 'Association between sleep duration and cognitive decline', *JAMA Network Open* 3 (9): e2013573. doi:10.1001/jamanetworkopen.2020.13573.

7: Being tired destroys your cognitive abilities

56 Lowrie, J. and Brownlow, H. (2020), 'The impact of sleep deprivation and alcohol on driving: A comparative study', *BMC Public Health*.

57 From correspondence with Prof. Steven Lockley at Harvard Medical School.

58 Fritz, J., et al. (2020), 'A chronobiological evaluation of the acute effects of daylight saving time on traffic accident risk', *Current Biology*.

59 Tefft, B. (2020), 'Acute sleep deprivation and culpable motor vehicle crash involvement', *Sleep*.

60 Wild, C., et al. (2019), 'Dissociable effects of self-reported daily sleep duration on high-level cognitive abilities', *Sleep*.

61 Barnes, C. M., et al. (2014), 'Sleep and moral awareness', *Journal of Sleep Research*.

62 Alkozei, A., et al. (2018), 'Chronic sleep restriction affects the association between implicit bias and explicit social decision making', *Sleep Health*.

8: Sleep is a kind of overnight therapy

63 Conte, F., et al. (2021), 'The effects of sleep quality on dream and waking emotions', *International Journal of Environmental Research and Public Health*.

64 Walker, M. and Ven der Helm, E. (2009), 'Overnight therapy? The role of sleep in emotional brain processing', *Psychological Bulletin*.

65 Jagannath, A., et al. (2017), 'The genetics of circadian rhythms, sleep and health', *Human Molecular Genetics*.

66 Foster, R. (2020), 'Sleep, circadian rhythms and health', *Interface Focus*.

67 Walker, M. (2009), 'The role of sleep in cognition and emotion', *Annals of the New York Academy of Sciences*.

68 Freeman, D., et al. (2017), 'The effects of improving sleep on mental health (OASIS): A randomised controlled trial with mediation analysis', *Lancet Psychiatry*.

69 Pace-Schott, E., et al. (2015), 'Effects of sleep on memory for conditioned fear and fear extinction', *Psychological Bulletin*.

9: How much sleep do you really need?

70 Rechtschaffen, A. (1989), 'Sleep deprivation in the rat: III. Total sleep deprivation', *Sleep*.

71 Foster, R. G. (2020), 'Sleep, circadian rhythms and health', *Interface Focus*.

72 Duffy, J., et al. (2015), 'Aging and circadian rhythms', *Sleep Medicine Clinics*.

73 Lockley, S. and Foster, R. (2012), *Sleep: A Very Short Introduction*, Oxford.

74 Cauter, E., Leproult, R. and Plat, L. (2000), 'Age-related changes in slow wave sleep and REM sleep and relationship with growth hormone and cortisol levels in healthy men', *JAMA*.

75 Gottlieb, D., et al. (2015), 'Novel loci associated with usual sleep duration:

The CHARGE consortium genome-wide association study', *Molecular Psychiatry*.

76 Xu, W., et al. (2020), 'Sleep problems and risk of all-cause cognitive decline or dementia: An updated systematic review and meta-analysis', *Journal of Neurology, Neurosurgery, and Psychiatry*.

77 Léger, D., et al. (2014), 'The risks of sleeping "too much": Survey of a national representative sample of 24671 adults (INPES Health Barometer), *PLOS One*.

78 *New Scientist* (2015), 'Late nights and lie-ins at the weekend are bad for your health'.

79 Lockley, S. and Foster, R. (2012), *Sleep: A Very Short Introduction*, Oxford.

80 Foster, R. G. (2020), 'Sleep, circadian rhythms and health', *Interface Focus*.

81 Ibid.

82 Ibid.

83 Walch, O., Cochran, A. and Forger, B. (2016), 'A global quantification of "normal" sleep schedules using smartphone data', *Science Advances*.

10: Tiredness can be all in the mind

84 Gavriloff, D., et al. (2018), 'Sham sleep feedback delivered via actigraphy biases daytime symptom reports in people with insomnia: Implications for insomnia disorder and wearable devices', *Journal of Sleep Research*.

85 Draganich, C. and Erdal, K. (2014), 'Placebo sleep affects cognitive functioning', *Journal of Experimental Psychology: Learning, Memory, and Cognition*.

86 Zavecz, Z., et al. (2020), 'The relationship between subjective sleep quality and cognitive performance in healthy young adults: Evidence from three empirical studies', *Scientific Reports*.

87 Lichtlein, K. (2017), 'Insomnia identity', *Behaviour Research and Therapy*.

88 McFarlane, F., et al. (2020), 'Auditory countermeasures for sleep inertia: Exploring the effect of melody and rhythm in an ecological context', *Clocks & Sleep*.

89 Hilditch, C. and McHill, A. (2019), 'Sleep inertia: current insights', *Nature and Science of Sleep*.

PART 3: EXERCISE
Introduction

90 WHO 2018 German Physical Activity Factsheet.

91 2018 Physical Activity Guidelines, Advisory Committee Scientific Report F3-29.

92 US 2016 National Health Interview Survey.

11: Exercise is one of the key ways to prevent dementia

93 Livingston, G., et al. (2020), 'Dementia prevention, intervention, and care: 2020 report of the Lancet Commission', *The Lancet*.

94 Wiley, J., et al. (2018), 'Leisure-time physical activity associates with cognitive decline', *Neurology*.

95 Ronan, L., et al. (2016), 'Obesity associated with increased brain age from midlife', *Neurobiology of Ageing*.

96 De Lucia, C., et al. (2020), 'Lifestyle mediates the role of nutrient-sensing pathways in cognitive aging: Cellular and epidemiological evidence', *Nature*.

97 www.ted.com (2015), 'You can grow new brain cells: Here's how'.

98 Lourenco, M. V., et al. (2019), 'Exercise-linked FNDC5/irisin rescues synaptic plasticity and memory defects in Alzheimer's models', *Nature Medicine*.

99 Colombe, S., et al. (2006), 'Aerobic exercise training increases brain volume in aging humans', *The Journals of Gerontology: Series A*.

100 www.hsph.harvard.edu (no date), 'Examples of moderate and vigorous physical activity'.

12: Exercise amps up your brain power

101 Hamilton, M., et al. (2012), 'Too little exercise and too much sitting: Inactivity physiology and the need for new recommendations on sedentary behavior', *Current Cardiovascular Risk Reports*.

102 Stimpson, N., et al. (2018), 'Joggin' the noggin: Towards a physiological understanding of exercise-induced cognitive benefits', *Neuroscience & Biobehavioral Reviews*.

103 Donnelly, J., et al. (2016), 'Physical activity, fitness, cognitive function, and academic achievement in children', *Medicine & Science in Sports & Exercise*.

104 Firth, J., et al. (2018), 'Grip strength is associated with cognitive performance in schizophrenia and the general population: A UK Biobank study of 476559 participants', *Schizophrenia Bulletin*.

105 Sternäng, O., et al. (2016), 'Grip strength and cognitive abilities: Associations in old age', *Journals of Gerontology: B*.

106 Fritz, N., et al. (2017), 'Handgrip strength as a means of monitoring progression of cognitive decline – a scoping review', *Ageing Research Reviews*.

13: Exercise can boost your mental wellbeing

107 Liao, Y., et al. (2015), 'The acute relationships between affect, physical feeling states, and physical activity in daily life: A review of current evidence', *Frontiers in Psychology*.

108 Chekroud, S., et al. (2018), 'Association between physical exercise and mental health in 1.2 million individuals in the USA between 2011 and 2015: A cross-sectional study', *Lancet Psychiatry*.

109 Mammen, G. and Faulkner, G. (2013), 'Physical activity and the prevention of depression: A systematic review of prospective studies', *American Journal of Preventive Medicine*.

110 Josefsson, T., et al. (2014), 'Physical exercise intervention in depressive disorders: Meta-analysis and systematic review', *Scandinavian Journal of Medicine & Science in Sports*.

111 2018 Physical Activity Guidelines, Advisory Committee Scientific Report F3-29.

112 Maddock, R. (2016), 'Acute modulation of cortical glutamate and GABA content by physical activity', *Journal of Neuroscience*.

113 Di Liegro, C. M., et al. (2019), 'Physical activity and brain health', *Genes*.

114 *New Scientist* (2018), 'How busting some moves on the dance floor is good for your brain'.

115 Paolucci, E. M., et al. (2018), 'Exercise reduces depression and inflammation but intensity matters', *Biological Psychology*.

14: Yoga can change your brain and calm the mind

116 *New York Times* (2020), 'Two Parents. Two Kids. Two Jobs. No Child Care'.

117 Yogaalliance.org (2016), 'Highlights from the 2016 Yoga in America study'.

118 Pascoe, M. C. and Bauer, I. E. (2015), 'A systematic review of randomised control trials on the effects of yoga on stress measures and mood', *Journal of Psychiatric Research*.

119 Park, C., et al. (2020), 'Exploring how different types of yoga change psychological resources and emotional well-being across a single session', *Complementary Therapies in Medicine*.

120 Desai, R., et al. (2015), 'Effects of yoga on brain waves and structural activation: A review', *Complementary Therapies in Clinical Practice*.

121 Pascoe, M. C. and Bauer, I. E. (2015), 'A systematic review of randomised control trials on the effects of yoga on stress measures and mood', *Journal of Psychiatric Research*.

122 Gothe, N., et al. (2014), 'The Effects of an 8-Week Hatha Yoga Intervention on Executive Function in Older Adults', *The Journals of Gerontology: Series A*.

123 Cowan, N., et al. (2013), 'Working memory underpins cognitive development, learning, and education', *Educational Psychology Review*.

124 Streeter, C., et al. (2010), 'Effects of yoga versus walking on mood, anxiety, and brain GABA levels: A randomized controlled MRS study', *Journal of Alternative and Complementary Medicine*.

125 Desai, R., et al. (2015), 'Effects of yoga on brain waves and structural activation: A review', *Complementary Therapies in Clinical Practice*.

126 Hölzel, B., et al. (2010), 'Stress reduction correlates with structural changes in the amygdala', *Social Cognitive and Affective Neuroscience*.

15: Be mindful of mindfulness

127 Van Dam, N., et al. (2017), 'Mind the hype: A critical evaluation and prescriptive agenda for research on mindfulness and meditation', *Perspectives on Psychological Science*.

128 Zeidan, F. and Vago, D. (2016), 'Mindfulness meditation-based pain relief: A mechanistic account', *Annals of the New York Academy of Sciences*.

129 Hoffman, S., et al. (2010), 'The effect of mindfulness-based therapy on anxiety and depression: A meta-analytic review', *Journal of Consulting and Clinical Psychology*.

130 Kuyken, W., et al. (2015), 'Effectiveness and cost-effectiveness of mindfulness-based cognitive therapy compared with maintenance antidepressant treatment in the prevention of depressive relapse or recurrence (PREVENT): A randomised controlled trial', *The Lancet*.

131 Wikipedia.

132 Techcrunch.com (2020), 'Headspace raises $93 million in equity and debt as it pursues clinical validation for mindfulness'.

133 Farias, M., et al. (2020), 'Adverse events in meditation practices and meditation-based therapies: A systematic review', *Acta Psychiatrica Scandinavica.*

PART 4: MENTAL EXERCISE
Introduction

134 Hampshire, A., et al. (2019), 'A large-scale, cross-sectional investigation into the efficacy of brain training', *Frontiers in Human Neuroscience.*

16: You can grow new brain cells

135 Kumar, A., et al. (2019), 'Adult neurogenesis in humans: A review of basic concepts, history, current research, and clinical implications', *Innovations in Clinical Neuroscience.*

136 Ninds.org (no date), 'Brain basics: The life and death of a neuron'.

137 Laham, B. J. and Gould, E. (2020), 'Plasticity in the adult brain', *Reference Module in Neuroscience and Biobehavioral Psychology.*

138 Eriksson, P., et al. (1998), 'Neurogenesis in the adult human hippocampus', *Nature Medicine.*

139 Boldrini, M., et al. (2018), 'Human hippocampal neurogenesis persists throughout aging', *Cell Stem Cell.*

140 Moreno-Jiménez, E. P., et al. (2019), 'Adult hippocampal neurogenesis is abundant in neurologically healthy subjects and drops sharply in patients with Alzheimer's disease', *Nature Medicine.*

141 von Bartheld, C. S. (2018), 'Myths and truths about the cellular composition of the human brain: A review of influential concepts', *Journal of Chemical Neuroanatomy.*

142 Bergmann, O. and Frisén, J. (2013), 'Why adults need new brain cells', *Neuroscience.*

17: Education protects your brain

143 *New Scientist* (2005), 'How brainpower can help you cheat old age'.

144 Ageuk.org.uk (2020), 'Cognitive reserve'.

145 Valenzuela, M., and Sachdev, P. (2006) 'Brain reserve and dementia: a systematic review', *Psychological Medicine.*

146 Wilson, R., et al. (2019), 'Education and cognitive reserve in old age', *Neurology.*

147 Lövdén, M., et al. (2020), 'Education and cognitive functioning across the life span', *Psychological Science in the Public Interest.*

148 Avila, J., et al. (2020), 'Education differentially contributes to cognitive reserve across racial/ethnic groups', *Alzheimer's and Dementia.*

149 Alzforum (2018), 'Intelligence matters more for brain reserve, but education helps'.

18: The bilingual brain boost

150 Antoniou, M. (2019), 'The advantages of bilingualism debate', *Annual Review of Linguistics.*

151 Peal, E. and Lambert, W. E. (1962), 'The relation of bilingualism to intelligence', *Psychological Monographs: General and Applied.*

152 Bialystok, E. (1988), 'Levels of bilingualism and levels of linguistic awareness', *Developmental Psychology*.

153 Prior, A. and Macwhinney, B. (2010), 'A bilingual advantage in task switching', *Bilingualism: Language and Cognition*.

154 Craik, F. I. M., Bialystok, E. and Freedman, M. (2010), 'Delaying the onset of Alzheimer disease', *Neurology*.

155 Much of this chapter was informed by an article I wrote for the *New Scientist*, titled 'Bilingual brain boost: Two tongues, two minds'.

156 Alladi, S., et al. (2013), 'Bilingualism delays age at onset of dementia, independent of education and immigration status', *Neurology*.

19: Music should be part of daily life

157 Criscuolo, A., Bonetti, L., Särkämö, T., Kliuchko, M. and Brattico, E. (2019), 'On the association between musical training, intelligence and executive functions in adulthood', *Frontiers in Psychology*.

158 Ibid.

159 Loui, P., et al. (2019), 'Musical instrument practice predicts white matter microstructure and cognitive abilities in childhood', *Frontiers in Psychology*.

160 Gooding, L., et al. (2015), 'Musical training and late-life cognition', *American Journal of Alzheimer's Disease & Other Dementias*.

161 Devere, R. (2017), 'Music and dementia: An overview', *Practical Neurology*.

162 Veghese, J., et al. (2003), 'Leisure activities and the risk of dementia in the elderly', *New England Journal of Medicine*.

163 Walsh, S., et al. (2021), 'Does playing a musical instrument reduce the incidence of cognitive impairment and dementia? A systematic review and meta-analysis', *Aging and Mental Health*.

164 Chaddock-Heyman, L., et al. (2021), 'Musical training and brain volume in older adults', *Brain Sciences*.

165 Leipold, S., Klein, C. and Jäncke, L. (2021), 'Musical expertise shapes functional and structural brain networks independent of absolute pitch ability', *Neuroscience*.

166 James, C., et al. (2020), 'Train the brain with music (TBM): Brain plasticity and cognitive benefits induced by musical training in elderly people in Germany and Switzerland, a study protocol for an RCT comparing musical instrumental practice to sensitization to music', *BMC Geriatrics*.

167 Devere, R. (2017), 'Music and dementia: An overview', *Practical Neurology*.

168 Krotinger, A. and Loui, P. (2021), 'Rhythm and groove as cognitive mechanisms of dance intervention in Parkinson's disease', *PLOS One*.

169 Tichko, P., et al. (2020), 'Integrating music-based interventions with Gamma-frequency stimulation: Implications for healthy ageing', *European Journal of Neuroscience*.

PART 5: SOCIAL LIFE
20: Marriage can protect you from dementia

170 Sommerlad, A., Ruegger, J., Singh-Manoux, A., et al. (2018), 'Marriage and risk of dementia: systematic review and meta-analysis of observational studies', *Journal of Neurology, Neurosurgery, and Psychiatry*.

171 Joung, I. M., Stronks, K., van de Mheen, H., et al. (1995), 'Health behaviours explain part of the differences in self-reported health associated with partner/marital status in The Netherlands', *Journal of Epidemiology and Community Health*.

172 Locke, H. J. and Wallace, K. M. (1959), 'Short marital adjustment and prediction tests: Their reliability and validity', *Marriage and Family Living*.

173 Holt-Lunstad, J., et al. (2008), 'Is there something unique about marriage? The relative impact of marital status, relationship quality, and network social support on ambulatory blood pressure and mental health', *Annals of Behavioral Medicine*.

174 Beadle, J. N. (2019), 'Leveraging the power of networks to support healthy aging', *The Journals of Gerontology*.

175 Blanchflower, D. G. and Clark, A. E. (2019), 'Children, unhappiness and family finances: Evidence from one million Europeans', *National Bureau of Economic Research*.

176 Becker, C., et al. (2019), 'Marriage, parenthood and social network: Subjective well-being and mental health in old age', *PLOS One*.

21: How loneliness changes your brain

177 Sutin, A., et al. (2020), 'Has loneliness increased during COVID-19? Comment on "'Loneliness: A signature mental health concern in the era of COVID-19'", *Psychiatry Research*.

178 Ortiz-Ospina, E. (2019), 'Is there a loneliness epidemic?' Retrieved from https://ourworldindata.org/loneliness-epidemic.

179 Coyle, C. and Dugan, E. (2012), 'Social isolation, loneliness and health among older adults', *Journal of Ageing and Health*.

180 *New Scientist* (2017), 'Feeling lonely? You're not on your own'. Retrieved from https://www.newscientist.com/article/mg23531351-900-feeling-lonely-youre-not-on-your-own/.

181 Richardson, T., et al. (2017), 'The relationship between loneliness and mental health in students', *Journal of Public Mental Health*.

182 Spithoven, A., et al. (2017), 'It is all in their mind: A review on information processing bias in lonely individuals', *Clinical Psychology Review*.

183 Hawkley, L. and Capitanio, J. (2016), 'Perceived social isolation, evolutionary fitness and health outcomes: A lifespan approach', *Philosophical Transactions of the Royal Society B*.

184 Cacioppo, S., et al. (2015), 'Loneliness: Clinical import and interventions', *Perspectives on Psychological Science*.

185 Pewresearch.org (2018), 'Americans unhappy with family, social or financial life are more likely to say they feel lonely'.

186 Masi, C. M., et al. (2011), 'A meta-analysis of interventions to reduce loneliness', *Personality and Social Psychology Review*.

187 Cole, S., et al. (2015), 'Loneliness, eudaimonia, and the human conserved transcriptional response to adversity', *Psychoneuroendocrinology*.

22: The healing power of pets

188 Robinson, A. S. (2019), 'Finding healing through animal companionship in Japanese animal cafés', *BMJ Medical Humanities*.

189 McNicholas, J., et al. (2005), 'Pet ownership and human health: A brief review of evidence and issues', *BMJ*.

190 Stoeckel, L., et al. (2014), 'Patterns of brain activation when mothers view their own child and dog: An fMRI study', *PLOS One*.

191 Centre for Mental Health (2018), 'The mental health impact of therapy dogs in prison'.

192 Theguardian.com (2020), 'Sanity, stability and stress-relief: Why our beloved pets have never been more important'.

193 Habri.org (2014), 'Family physician survey'.

194 *New Scientist* (2018), 'Why emotional support animals may be a waste of time'.

195 Hughes, M. (2019), 'Companion animals and health in older populations: A systematic review', *Clinical Gerontologist*.

196 Yerbury, R. M. and Lukey, S. J. (2021), 'Human–animal interactions: Expressions of wellbeing through a "nature language"', *Animals*.

23: The mood-boosting benefits of light and dark

197 Zee, P. C. (2015), 'Circadian clocks: Implication for health and disease', *Sleep Medicine Clinics*.

198 Bedrosian, T. and Nelson, R. J. (2017), 'Timing of light exposure affects mood and brain circuits', *Translational Psychiatry*.

199 Lee, E. E., et al. (2020), 'Daily and seasonal variation in light exposure among the Old Order Amish', *International Journal of Environmental Research and Public Health*.

200 BBC Future (2018), 'What I learned by living without artificial light'.

201 Ibid.

202 Münch, M., et al. (2016), 'Blue-enriched morning light as a countermeasure to light at the wrong time: Effects on cognition, sleepiness, sleep, and circadian phase', *Neuropsychobiology*.

203 Chang, A.-M., et al. (2015), 'Evening use of light-emitting eReaders negatively affects sleep, circadian timing, and next-morning alertness', *PNAS*.

24: Nature is good for mental health

204 Alcock, I., et al. (2014), 'Longitudinal effects on mental health of moving to greener and less green urban areas', *Environmental Science*.

205 United Nations (2018), 'World urbanization prospects: The 2018 revision'. Retrieved from https://population.un.org/wup/Publications/Files/WUP2018-Report.pdf.

206 White, M., et al. (2013), 'Would you be happier living in a greener urban area? A fixed-effects analysis of panel data', *Psychological Science*.

207 Berman, M. G., et al. (2008), 'The cognitive benefits of interacting with nature', *Psychological Science*.

208 White, M. L., et al. (2020), 'Nature contact, nature connectedness and associations with health, wellbeing and pro-environmental behaviours', *Journal of Environmental Psychology*.

209 Alcock, I., et al. (2020), 'Associations between pro-environmental behaviour and neighbourhood nature, nature visit frequency and nature appreciation: Evidence from a nationally representative survey in England', *Environment International*.

PART 6: HEALTHY BODY, HEALTHY MIND
25: Inflammation can mess with your mind

210 Cox, A., et al. (2015), 'Obesity, inflammation, and the gut microbiota', *Lancet: Diabetes & Endocrinology*.

211 *Nature* (2021), '"Inflammation clock" can reveal body's biological age'.

212 *New Scientist* (2015), 'An inflamed brain may be a hidden cause of depression'.

213 Lee, C.-H. and Giuliani, F. (2019), 'The role of inflammation in depression and fatigue', *Frontiers in Immunology*.

214 Bai, S., et al. (2019), 'Efficacy and safety of anti-inflammatory agents for the treatment of major depressive disorder: A systematic review and meta analysis of randomised controlled trials', *Journal of Neurology, Neurosurgery, and Psychiatry*.

215 Miller, A. and Pariante, C. (2020), 'Trial failures of anti-inflammatory drugs in depression', *Lancet Psychiatry*.

26: To help avoid Alzheimer's, take care of your teeth

216 *New York Times* (2021), 'House Committees Demand F.D.A. Records on Alzheimer's Drug Approval'.

217 *New Scientist* (2019), 'We may finally know what causes Alzheimer's – and how to stop it'.

218 Domini, S., et al. (2019), '*Porphyromonas gingivalis* in Alzheimer's disease brains: Evidence for disease causation and treatment with small-molecule inhibitors', *Science Advances*.

219 Harding, A., Robinson, S., Crean, S.-J. and Singhrao, S. K. (2017), 'Can better management of periodontal disease delay the onset and progression of Alzheimer's disease?', *Journal of Alzheimer's Disease*.

220 Chen, C.-K., Wu, Y.-T. and Chang, Y.-C. (2017), 'Periodontal inflammatory disease is associated with the risk of Parkinson's disease: A population-based retrospective matched-cohort study', *PeerJ*.

27: Hearing loss is linked to dementia

221 Lin, F. R., et al. (2011), 'Hearing loss and incident dementia', *Aging and Mental Health*.

222 Byeon, G., et al. (2021), 'Dual sensory impairment and cognitive impairment in the Korean longitudinal elderly cohort', *Neurology*.

223 Lin, F. R. and Albert, M. (2014), 'Hearing loss and dementia – who's listening?', *Aging and Mental Health*.

224 Alzheimer's.co.uk (2021), 'Wearing hearing aid may help protect brain in later life'.

225 www.hopkinsmedicine.org (no date available), 'The hidden risks of hearing loss'.

PART 7: THE INFLUENCE OF YOU
28: Your personality affects your mental health

226 Steiger, M., et al. (2021), 'Changing personality traits with the help of a digital personality change intervention', *PNAS*.

227 Lamers, M., et al. (2012), 'Differential relationships in the association of the Big Five personality traits with positive mental health and psychopathology', *Journal of Research in Personality*.

228 Williams, P., et al. (2009), 'Openness to experience and stress regulation', *Journal of Research in Personality*.

229 Curran, T. and Hill, A. P. (2019), 'Perfectionism is increasing over time: A meta-analysis of birth cohort differences from 1989 to 2016', *Psychological Bulletin*.

230 Smith, M., et al. (2021), 'Is perfectionism a vulnerability factor for depressive symptoms, a complication of depressive symptoms, or both? A meta-analytic test of 67 longitudinal studies', *Clinical Psychology Review*.

231 Theconversation.com (2018), 'How perfectionism became a hidden epidemic among young people'.

232 Olsson, L., et al. (2021), 'Do athlete and coach performance perfectionism predict athlete burnout?', *European Journal of Sport Science*.

233 Srivastava, S., John, O. P., Gosling, S. D. and Potter, J. (2003), 'Development of personality in early and middle adulthood: Set like plaster or persistent change?', *Journal of Personality and Social Psychology*.

234 Asselmann, E. and Specht, J. (2020), 'Testing the social investment principle around childbirth: Little evidence for personality maturation before and after becoming a parent', *European Journal of Personality*.

235 *New Scientist* (2017), 'Your true self: How your personality changes throughout life'.

236 Hudson, N. W. and Fraley, R. C. (2015), 'Volitional personality trait change: Can people choose to change their personality traits?', *Journal of Personality and Social Psychology*.

237 Nagel, M., et al. (2018), 'Meta-analysis of genome-wide association studies for neuroticism in 449,484 individuals identifies novel genetic loci and pathways', *Nature Genetics*.

238 Steiger, M., et al. (2021), 'Changing personality traits with the help of a digital personality change intervention', *PNAS*.

239 Hudson, N. W. and Fraley, R. C. (2016), 'Changing for the better? Longitudinal associations between volitional personality change and psychological well-being', *Personality and Social Psychology Bulletin*.

240 *New Scientist* (2019), 'The misunderstood personality trait that is causing anxiety and stress'.

241 Nace.co.uk (2020), 'How perfectionistic is your classroom?'

29: Stress doesn't have to be bad

242 Salleh, M. R. (2008), 'Life event, stress and illness', *Malaysian Journal of Medical Sciences*.

243 Jinshil Hyun, M. A., et al. (2018), 'Waking up on the wrong side of the bed: The effects of stress anticipation on working memory in daily life',

The Journals of Gerontology: Series B.

244 *New Scientist* (2020), 'Don't stress: The scientific secrets of people who keep cool heads'.

245 Sliter, M., Kale, A. and Yuan, Z. (2013), 'Is humor the best medicine? The buffering effect of coping humor on traumatic stressors in firefighters', *Journal of Organizational Behavior.*

246 Tagalidou, N., et al. (2018), 'Feasibility of a humor training to promote humor and decrease stress in a subclinical sample: A single-arm pilot study', *Frontiers in Psychology.*

247 Zander-Schellenberg, T., et al. (2020), 'Does laughing have a stress-buffering effect in daily life? An intensive longitudinal study', *PLOS One.*

248 *New Scientist* (2020), 'Stress early in life can make a child's brain more like an adult's'.

249 *Harvard Business Review* (2015), 'Stress can be a good thing if you know how to use it'.

250 Crum, A., et al. (2013), 'Rethinking stress: The role of mindsets in determining the stress response', *Personality, Processes and Individual Differences.*

30: How to form healthy habits

251 Wood, W., Quinn, J. M. and Kashy, D. A. (2002), 'Habits in everyday life: Thought, emotion, and action', *Journal of Personality and Social Psychology.*

252 *New Scientist* (2016), 'How to master your habits and take control of your life'.

253 Thomson, H. (2021), *This Book Could Fix Your Life.*

254 Howe, M., et al. (2011), 'Habit learning is associated with major shifts in frequencies of oscillatory activity and synchronized spike firing in striatum', *PNAS.*

255 Smith, K. S. and Graybiel, A. M. (2016), 'Habit formation', *Dialogues in Clinical Neuroscience.*

256 https://www.newscientist.com/article/mg24332400-700-how-to-trick-your-mind-to-break-bad-habits-and-reach-your-goals/.

257 Fournier, M., et al. (2017), 'Effects of circadian cortisol on the development of a health habit', *Health Psychology.*

258 Lally, P., et al. (2009), 'How are habits formed: Modelling habit formation in the real world', *European Journal of Social Psychology.*

259 Van der Weiden, A., et al. (2021), 'How to form good habits? A longitudinal field study on the role of self-control in habit formation', *Frontiers in Psychology.*

260 MIT News (2018), 'Distinctive brain pattern helps habits form'.

261 Keller, J., et al. (2021), 'Habit formation following routine-based versus time-based cue planning: A randomized controlled trial', *Health Psychology.*

Acknowledgements

First of all, thank you to Jo Stansall for coming to me with this book idea in the first place, and for your calm and patience yet again, as I grappled with the reality of writing it during the throes of a pandemic. Thank you also to Gabriella Nemeth for all your work on getting the manuscript ready.

A huge thank you to all the scientists who have taken the time to speak to me for this book and over the years on subject matter that has informed it, in particular Thomas Bak, Matthew Walker, Sandrine Thuret, Russel Foster, Alia Crum, Charles Hillman, Psyche Loui, Herman Pontzer, Steven Lockley and June Andrews. Apologies to anyone I have forgotten.

Helen Thomson, Melissa Hogenboom, Tiffany O'Callaghan, Jess Griggs, Rowan Hooper, thanks for your amazing editorial advice and general support, and a special thank you to those who read and commented on drafts: Chris Simms for your excellent eye, my dad Nicholas de Lange for your thoughtful comments, and Hana Ros for your neuroscience know-how.

Many of the themes in this book are subjects I have written about or edited for *New Scientist*, so I owe a huge debt of gratitude to my colleagues over the years and all the writers who I have edited on these topics. A special thank you to Emily Wilson for supporting me even though I ignored your wise advice that my evenings might be more enjoyably spent doing yoga.

Thank you to the rest of my wonderful family, especially my mum Patricia for taking such good care of my children so often as deadlines loomed, as well as to my in-laws Dr and Mrs Jha.

Amelie and Remy – thank you for the cuddles, and the perspective. And Alok, in the past couple of years the world spun off its axis, and this book hasn't made things any easier. Thank you for being the calm in the storm. Your pragmatism and cool-headed advice has seen me through (along with the late-night wine and ice cream). I've yet to meet a better brain.

Index

Diagrams and maps are shown in *italics*.